Praise for *Musical Truth*

WINNER
LONGLIS

A *The* 1 ... ...ies
Mus. ⌐ook of the Year

'**Engaging and accomplished** . . .
perfectly judged for young readers.'
The Guardian

'It's not just **a vital book**, but a killer playlist too.'
The Sunday Times

'Boakye is **a special talent** and *Musical
Truth* . . . deserves to be read widely.'
Books for Keeps

'**Fantastic.**'
Clash Magazine

'**Clever and accessible.**'
Patrice Lawrence, author of *Eight
Pieces of Silva* and *Orangeboy*

'An **incredible** piece of work.'
Kofi Smiles, BBC Radio presenter

'Thorough and inspiring . . . Not just **essential reading** for older children and teens (and adults!) but essential listening too.'
BookTrust

'A **unique** book . . . Accessible, lively and informative.'
School Reading List

'Needs to be in every home, classroom and library.'
Rashmi Sirdeshpande, author of
How to Change the World

'**Ground-breaking** musical journey . . . that will also deeply touch your soul.'
Candid Cocoa

'Highly accessible and creatively written.'
Jasmine, aged 17, *Books up North*

'**I loved it**, took me down yesteryear!'
Alex Wheatle, author of *Cane Warriors*

'A book that will inform, educate, encourage.'
Just Read It

Musical World

Modern World History as You've Never Heard it Before

JEFFREY BOAKYE
Art by Ngadi Smart

faber

First published in the UK in 2023
by Faber & Faber Limited
The Bindery, 51 Hatton Garden
London, EC1N 8HN
faber.co.uk

Typeset by M Rules in Mr Eaves
This font has been specially chosen to support reading

Printed and bound by CPI Group (UK) Ltd, Croydon, CR0 4YY

A CIP record for this book
is available from the British Library

ISBN 978-0-571-37749-7

MIX
Paper | Supporting
responsible forestry
FSC® C171272

Printed and bound in the UK on FSC® certified paper in line with our continuing
commitment to ethical business practices, sustainability and the environment.
For further information see faber.co.uk/environmental-policy

2 4 6 8 10 9 7 5 3 1

For anyone seeking unity in a world of music.
This is for us.

Playlist

*Listen to the songs on our YouTube playlist at
musicalworldplaylist.co.uk.*

Introduction

When I listen to music, it feels like I'm time-travelling to places I've never been to, and speaking to people I've never met. In a really good way, music throws you into history, inviting you to dive into an ocean of sounds and come up for air feeling totally refreshed.

Like millions of people all over the world, music has been a constant part of my life, helping me to understand the world I was born into. I've been exploring music since I was a child, listening to songs much older than me or listening out for new styles that hint at the future.

In this way, music isn't just about having a good time.

It can be a conversation between different generations. It can describe and challenge the injustices of our world. It can also celebrate heroic people. It can tell us the stories of the world, through infinite possibilities of sound put together to express the biggest ideas and the deepest emotions. That's what this book is all about.

There are so many stories in our shared human history and music has the ability to tell them all – in unique and surprising ways. Get ready for a three-hundred-year trip through time, making stops in countries all over the world, meeting fascinating people with amazing lives. We'll see how ancient traditions continue into the modern day. We'll explore the birth and growth of new styles of music, invented at different times, in various places, by many people. We'll find out about moments in history that define us all, offering lessons to learn from and inspiration for the future.

We'll also meet people who have suffered and struggled to fit in. Communities who have had their power taken away by a world that can be cruel. And we'll see how people have used music to express themselves and show the whole world who they really are.

My last book about music is called *Musical Truth*, all about the history of black communities in modern

Britain. *This* book looks even wider and further, exploring the realities of communities all over the world and taking a global look at the struggles people have faced over time. Because of this, a lot of these pages will be about *power* and the way that groups of people have tried to control other groups. The world can be a very unfair place – something that we can hear in music, throughout time. But for all the struggle and hardship, there is joy and celebration too.

So. Welcome to *Musical World* – a musical journey through history that will help us to understand who we are and how we got here. Are you ready?

Let's go.

'Ah, vous dirai-je, Maman'

Unknown (c. 1740s)

Question: How does music travel through time?

I think you've heard this one before.

In fact, there's a good chance that you've actually sung it, on your own or with large groups of people, *many, many* times in your life so far, even if you never knew where it came from.

Because that's the thing about music: it exists in the air. A song can travel invisibly for miles, for years, throughout time.

5

The melody in 'Ah, vous dirai-je, Maman' (Ah, shall I tell you, Mama) is one of the most famous melodies of all time, and most of us will have first encountered it as very young children. In English, it's the tune to the alphabet song that helps children to learn their ABCs, as well as famous nursery rhymes such as 'Baa, Baa, Black Sheep' and 'Twinkle, Twinkle, Little Star'. That's part of the reason why this song is so comforting to listen to. It makes you think of lullabies and childhood. If you grew up in an English-speaking country and learned English as an infant, there's a good chance that you couldn't even read this sentence if it had not been for this song.

As you can probably tell from the title, this song is originally French. It is thought that the melody could go back as far as 1740, made up by someone somewhere in the French countryside, with the lyrics added many years later. In the 1700s, many countries in Europe were becoming increasingly powerful in the world at large. France was no exception. The reign of King Louis XIV lasted from 1643 to 1715, which is one of the longest in history. During this time, France became a dominant European force led by a powerful monarchy.

This would all change towards the end of the eighteenth century, when a revolution took place that overthrew the monarchy completely, making France a republic in 1792.

One of the most famous things to come out of the French Revolution was the phrase *liberté, égalité, fraternité*, which translates as liberty (or freedom), equality (everyone being treated the same) and brotherhood (the idea that we are all connected as family). It's a noble sentiment and one that many people will strive for. However, for reasons that we shall explore in this book, liberty, equality and familyhood is something that humans often find quite hard to achieve. Take a look at the world at any given time and you'll find, somewhere, the exact opposite of these three ideals.

The French monarchy didn't continue beyond the revolution, but French music and culture certainly did. The tune for 'Ah, vous dirai-je, Maman' is one good example of it. It proved to be so popular that many decades after it was first created, a young composer from Austria (aged about twenty-five) composed a piece for the piano based on its melody. His name was Wolfgang Amadeus Mozart, and he is one of the most famous composers of all time. One version of the story says that Mozart probably used his variations to teach his students how to play the piano, probably because the tune is so beautifully simple.

Today, the melody is well over two hundred and fifty years old and counting, but it has survived happily, reborn in different places through different times. Highlights include the German Christmas carol 'Morgen kommt der Weihnachtsmann' (Tomorrow Comes Santa Claus), the Hungarian Christmas carol 'Hull a pelyhes fehér hó' (Fluffy White Snow Is Falling), the Dutch nursery rhyme 'Altijd is Kortjakje' (Kortjakje Is Always Sick), the Spanish 'Campanita del lugar' (Little Town Bell) and the Turkish 'Daha Dün Annemizin' (Just Yesterday).

We will always need songs that speak to the child inside us, because that's how we all start out: as children. Innocent and ready to learn . . .

This song is a perfect example of how something as simple as a tune can travel through time, soothing millions of children (even while revolutions are raging on in the background). But as we shall soon see, a tune can do much more than sing us to sleep and help us remember the alphabet. It can even help us to create whole countries.

'God Save the King'

Unknown (c. 1744)

Question: When does a song make you proud to be you?

You hear them at the start of large sports competitions, in formal ceremonies, sometimes at big gatherings, but what is the purpose of a national anthem? Where do they come from? And why do people sing them with one hand on their heart and their eyes closed?

The whole point of a national anthem is to make people feel proud of their country. That's why you might have seen sports stars almost crying with emotion when they sing an anthem before an important sporting event. It raises the question: what's so good about any particular country that should make you want to sing a song about it?

One answer is that countries, or nations, offer us a strong sense of identity. Often, we define ourselves by the country that we were born in, because this is where our language, our food, our culture and histories come from. It's why the question *where are you from?* gets asked so often, especially to people who look or sound like they might not be from the country they are in.

That's one of the problems with national identity. Yes, it's something to be proud of and celebrate, but it can also be divisive. And when different countries have different levels of power and influence, overly strong nationalist feelings can start to cause problems. Think about what can happen when two or more countries get into a disagreement and end up in serious conflict with each other. We call them 'wars', and they have been responsible for some of the most tragic waste of human life in our shared history. (It's no accident that military traditions often include soldiers singing the national anthem together.)

National anthems have not been around forever. In fact, they are thought to have originated in Europe only a few hundred years ago. The first and oldest one is a song from Holland in the 1570s called 'Het Wilhelmus', but that didn't officially become the Dutch national anthem until 1932.

The popularity of national anthems throughout the world has a lot to do with the growing popularity of *nationalism* as an idea. By the time you got to the eighteenth and nineteenth centuries, national identity, as an idea, was becoming fixed in many different European countries. In world history, European countries are not very old. In fact, none of the top ten oldest countries on record are even in Europe, and eight of these gained sovereignty in the BC era (meaning 'Before Christ', or before the common era, which means before we started counting the years in numbers). The reason that European countries took the lead in the spread of national anthems is because these countries were becoming more powerful. Countries such as Germany, Spain and France were establishing themselves as new global powers. The self-belief needed to go around the world building an empire also needed a soundtrack. This might explain why Spain and France have national anthems that have a marching, military rhythm. These songs were deliberately powerful.

One of the most powerful empires of all time was the

British Empire. It was in the 1700s that Britain used its wealth, its army and its navy to cruelly conquer other lands, setting itself up as the most powerful nation in the world. It was a *colonial* power too, meaning that it won its power by entering and controlling other nations (its *colonies*), while also fighting with its rivals (like Spain and France) in order to stay on top.

'God Save the King' is a simple tune. It has a measured, churchy melody that builds slowly to a very grand-sounding finish. It's not about the empire, or about Britain's powerful trading habits. It has lyrics designed to flatter the king or queen of England at the time. When it was first performed, it wasn't in battle or when subjugating other lands: it was in a theatre in London, and it was intended to make the reigning monarch happy. And at one point, 'God Save the King' was the national anthem for every single country in the British Empire, meaning that millions of people who had never even been to Britain would have sung it – because they had to.

Wherever you find power, injustice is never far behind. In order to build their empires, colonising European countries put themselves at the front of the conversation. Their music was a huge part of this. The legacy of European imperialism can be heard in the fact that national anthems all kind of sound the same. They are almost always European-sounding hymns (church songs) or marches (military songs), played on European instruments. Even now, with many postcolonial countries having won their independence, the anthems they sing are often an echo of their European colonisers. Historically, colonialism is responsible for many, many horrific acts carried out by European countries who wanted control.

Control. It's a powerful word, isn't it? It's what countries throughout history have often tried to win. The ability to control people, places, situations and stories. When you look at history, this need for control has caused some of the worst conflicts in all humanity, when different nations end up clashing in their search for power. At its worst, this goes way beyond arguments with words and can lead to violence, fighting and war. I'm forty-one years old – which is pretty young compared to the age of the human species. And yet in every year that I have been alive, there has been violent conflict between different groups of people somewhere on the planet. One of the biggest reasons for these conflicts is often the idea of national differences: us against them, you against me, this country against that country. When in reality, we're all in this together.

I want you to think about this the next time you hear a national anthem. Think about the pride it is supposed to make you feel, and how this pride can so easily slip into a feeling of competition over who is better than who. Think about the long and complex histories of different countries, running to the soundtrack of national anthems that pre-date all of us. Think about what we believe in when we sing these songs with our hands on our hearts and a tear in our eye. And think about whether or not we really need these feelings as we go forward, as a species.

It's not an easy question, but definitely one that we need to come back to when our differences feel bigger than our similarities.

'Nkosi Sikelel' iAfrika' (God Bless Africa)

Enoch Sontonga (1897)

Question: Can one song bring a whole continent together?

Sometimes, a table is not just a table.

Sometimes, a table is power.

Sometimes, having 'a seat at the table' means having the power to make big decisions that affect other people – without their permission or consent.

Between 1884 and 1885, decisions like this were being made about the whole continent of Africa by groups of men who were sitting around a very big table indeed. It was called the Berlin Conference: a meeting of fourteen countries that were all looking for a piece of Africa to claim as their own. The reasons for this were simple: power, control and greed. Africa, as a continent, is full of valuable natural resources, and in the nineteenth century, emerging colonial powers were keen to take their share. The European nations present at the Berlin Conference were:

- Germany
- Austria-Hungary
- Belgium
- Denmark
- Spain
- France
- United Kingdom
- Italy
- Netherlands
- Portugal
- Russia
- Sweden–Norway
- Ottoman Empire

The only non-European country in attendance was the United States of America, which was a former colony of the United Kingdom (and therefore led by white Americans).

Let's think about all this for a second.

Africa: the second-largest continent on Earth, the place where all humanity originated, home to dozens of different groups and separate countries, was about to be carved up by a small selection of European countries purely for economic gain. When those men sat down around the table to argue who should get what, it was a moment of greed and great cruelty. (And it's worth noting that these were exclusively men, not women, because the world in 1884 was even more sexist than it is now.)

The Berlin Conference left Africa in a broken state. Whole countries were put under colonial rule, and would remain so for years and years to come. My parents are from a country called Ghana in west Africa. Ghana was once colonised by Britain. Under British imperial rule, it was given the name the Gold Coast, named after one of its most valuable resources – gold. It wasn't until 1957 that the Gold Coast would become independent. That's when the name 'Ghana' came about, when my parents were still very young children.

There are dozens of stories like this connected to African nations, illustrating how European countries gave themselves so much power over people from Africa.

In 1897, this was the situation that a young man called Enoch Sontonga found himself in. Enoch was a composer, but he had also been a teacher and the leader of a choir at a church in South Africa. At the age of twenty-four, he wrote a song called 'Nkosi Sikelel' iAfrika', which would go on to become one of the most famous songs in African history.

Enoch's song was a hymn. Its title translates from the original Xhosa language into 'Lord bless Africa'. It's a soaring but poignant song that sounds somehow triumphant and reflective at the very same time. It doesn't sound like a song you would march into battle with, or pure flattery for a king or queen. It sounds like a prayer.

Now, 'Nkosi Sikelel' iAfrika' is widely thought of as a kind of anthem for all of Africa. It has been used as symbol of liberation for the whole continent. I myself have heard it played long and loud in Ghanaian churches. Different versions of it have been taken as anthems for a number of African countries, including Zambia, Namibia, Zimbabwe and Tanzania. In an important sense, this song represents African resilience and celebration in a world that was very much treating African nations as less worthy of respect than dominant European ones. Racism had long ago created the idea of black people being lesser than white people, and Africa is home to many millions of black people.

In 1948, just over fifty years after Enoch Sontonga wrote his song, South Africa entered into a situation of racial segregation, whereby black and white South Africans were legally not allowed to mix together. This period was known as *apartheid*, meaning 'separateness' or 'aparthood', and it lasted all the way until the 1990s. Under apartheid, South Africans were put into the racial groups of Black, White, Coloured and Indian, based entirely on the colour of their skin, with white South Africans having the most rights. Between 1960 and 1983, three and a half million black South Africans were forced out of their homes to live in segregated neighbourhoods. This was an act of great cruelty that proved just how racist the government had become.

It wouldn't be until the early 1990s that apartheid would finally come to an end, after three long years of discussion between the government and different political groups, probably sitting around a very big table. This led to South Africa's first-ever multiracial elections in 1994, where black politicians were allowed to take part and everyone, of any colour, was allowed to vote. This led to the election of South Africa's first-ever black president – a man who spoke Xhosa, like Enoch Sontonga, and had been imprisoned for twenty-seven years for fighting against apartheid. His name was Nelson Mandela, and in 1994 he decided that 'Nkosi Sikelel' iAfrika' would be part of a new joint national anthem for a country that had been ripped apart for so long.

To this day, South Africa is a harsh example of how racism can leave scars on a country's history, and it's powerful to think that a simple song could be part of the healing process.

'Hava Nagila'

Moshe Nathanson (1918)

Question: How can music bring joy, through pain?

In 1918, a twelve-year-old boy was given a challenge by his choirmaster at school in Jerusalem. The challenge was to come up with words to accompany an old tune from many years before. The boy decided to go to the Bible for inspiration. He found a bit that said:

> *This is the day that the Lord has made*
> *Let us rejoice and be glad in it*

and added these words to the music. But the words he used weren't in English. They were in Hebrew, an ancient language from Israel dating back to the tenth century BCE (before the common era, before Jesus Christ is thought to be born). In Hebrew, the words *Let us rejoice* translate into *Hava nagila*, which is what young Moshe Nathanson's song became known as.

'Hava Nagila' sounds older than it is because it's so traditional in style, using very traditional instruments and ancient-sounding folk melodies. Its melody originally comes from a region that is now known as Ukraine, where it would have been used as a prayer without words. It's a good example of how a song can become 'timeless'.

Over time, 'Hava Nagila' became a very special part of Jewish culture, deeply connected with the history of Jewish people. You'll hear it at weddings and in coming-of-age ceremonies for young Jewish people, called bat mitzvahs (for girls) or bar mitzvahs (for boys). For Jewish people, 'Hava Nagila' is a time-tested song of celebration. Even if you've never heard it before, take one listen and you know it's time to celebrate. It's upbeat and excited, with a swaying, bubbly rhythm, and instruments that sound like they're having a party all of their own. It's fun too, inviting you to stand up and dance.

But for Jewish communities over time, the reality of the situation is far heavier.

Throughout history, Jewish people have suffered persecution and discrimination simply for being Jewish. It's a cruel, senseless type of racism known as antisemitism, targeting Jewish communities for hundreds of years. The causes of antisemitism are rooted in hatred, and over time, Jewish people have been targeted for different reasons:

- Religious reasons (where Jews are blamed for the death of Jesus Christ)
- Economic reasons (where Jews are stereotyped as being obsessed with money)
- Political reasons (where Jews are seen as revolutionary troublemakers)
- Social reasons (where Jews are treated as unsociable and not worth mixing with)
- Racist reasons (where Jews are seen as an inferior race with dehumanised physical features)

When you add it all up, antisemitism doesn't make any sense. But it led to one of the most appalling acts of cruelty in human history – the deliberate killing of Jewish men, women and children in a mass murder known as the Holocaust.

When you study the Holocaust at school, you learn about how Jewish communities were persecuted as part of Nazi Germany. You learn about the beliefs of Adolf Hitler, the leader of the Nazi party in the 1930s, who decided that Jews were inferior to other groups. You learn about the evil process of forcing Jews out of their homes and making them live in awful *ghettos*, before sending them away to live in concentration camps, stripped of their possessions and separated from their families. Then you learn about the systematic murder of Jewish people, first by firing squads and, eventually, in specially designed gas chambers.

Between 1939 and 1945, it is believed that six million Jewish people were murdered in this way.

The Holocaust is a stain on humanity. It is a genocide that should never have happened, reminding us of how evil humans can be. For this reason, an international Holocaust Memorial Day is held each year on 27 January, where the whole world is invited to remember the six million Jewish people who were killed. It also invites us to remember other groups who faced Nazi persecution at the time, including Roma and Sinti communities, Slavic people from Poland and Russia, and people of African descent. Other targeted groups included people who disagreed with Nazi ideas, gay people, and those who were thought to be 'disabled', either mentally or physically.

We're now a long, long way from the celebrations that opened this chapter. We're now talking about the most senseless loss of human life at a scale that is barely imaginable. We're talking about *genocide*, a crime where groups of people are stripped of all their human rights and targeted for cruel treatment and murder.

It happened to Jewish people in Nazi Germany.

It happened in 1970s Cambodia, when a political party called the Khmer Rouge killed millions of people in minority groups.

It happened in Rwanda in 1994, when conflict between two ethnic groups led to the murder of a million innocent people in only one hundred days.

It happened in Bosnia in 1995, when eight thousand Bosnian Muslims were killed in a period of seventy-two hours, their bodies hidden in mass graves.

It happened to millions of black Africans between the sixteenth and nineteenth centuries, taken from their homes and forced into slavery by white Europeans.

It's happening right now in Darfur, north-east

Africa, where ongoing civil war has led to the deaths of hundreds of thousands of people.

The power of a song like 'Hava Nagila' lies in its words: *let's rejoice*. For all the pain and suffering in Jewish history (and the ongoing antisemitism faced by Jewish communities globally, every day), there remains a spirit of joy, community and strength. After the end of the Second World War (and the decline of the Nazi regime) in the 1950s, non-Jewish artists began recording 'Hava Nagila'. One of the most famous was a black American superstar called Harry Belafonte. At one point, he found himself singing it in Germany to an audience of young Germans, only a few years after the war:

'It hit me kind of hard that here I was, an African American, an American, standing in Germany, which a decade earlier had been responsible for mass murder, these young German kids singing this Hebrew song of rejoicing . . . And I got very emotional.'

This book was never going to be an easy book to write, and it won't always be easy to read. But just because the truth of human history is full of pain and evil, we shouldn't look away from it. The Hebrew lyrics of 'Hava Nagila' tell us to 'rejoice' and 'be happy'. In a world like ours, joy, happiness and peace have to be the most important goals of all.

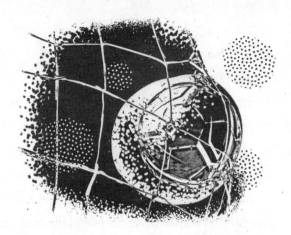

'Nessun Dorma'

from *Turandot* by Giacomo Puccini (1926)

Question: Does music help us to understand different cultures?

I'll admit it: I'm not a big fan of football. Which is perhaps unusual because football is one of the most popular sports in the whole world. It's played by millions of people across every continent, with thousands of hours devoted to following teams and watching groups of twenty-two people (usually men) chasing a ball full of air for ninety minutes at a time. Thankfully, things are changing and women's football is beginning to get the recognition it deserves. In July 2022, the UEFA Women's Euro 2022 final took place between England and Germany, attracting a crowd of more than 87,000 people (a record for any European Championship final).

Of course, I can't avoid football. Even though I don't support a team, and I hardly ever play, I frequently find myself getting swept away by big football events, screaming at the television and jumping up and down when someone scores a goal.

I'm talking about the World Cup. Every four years since 1930, the footballing world kicks into action with one of the biggest sporting events on the planet, where teams from almost every country on the planet go head to head to see who can kick a ball the best. It's terribly exciting. A chance to support your nation and join in the festivities.

1990 was a World Cup year, and it was one of the first World Cups that I can properly remember. I was eight. It was thrilling, seeing the whole world come alive in sport and competition. I found myself supporting England (that's where I live), and they did quite well, reaching the semi-finals against West Germany. Spoiler alert: England didn't win. It went to extra time and then penalties, which England lost. Then West Germany went on to win in the final, one nil, against Argentina. Congratulations.

The 1990 World Cup was held in Italy, which begins to explain why 'Nessun Dorma' became part of the soundtrack for the event. 'Nessun Dorma' is a piece of music from an opera called *Turandot*, written by an Italian composer called Puccini in 1926. An opera is a kind of musical story in which all the characters sing their thoughts and words on a very grand, dramatic stage. Operas originate from Italy near the end of the sixteenth century – before the first songs mentioned in this book.

As a child, I was swept away by 'Nessun Dorma'. I remember watching it being sung by a huge man with a huge voice called Luciano Pavarotti. It soared. It was as powerful as a jet engine but as graceful as a swan, full of drama and passion. It felt like a goal being scored at the last minute, backed by a sweeping orchestral soundscape and a chorus of strings that could make you want to cry. Looking back, I can see why the television controllers thought that this music would be a good accompaniment for the greatest sporting event in the world. It was breathtaking.

Like a lot of people, I never stopped to think about

where 'Nessun Dorma' came from. I had no idea that it came from *Turandot*, all about princes and princesses and dragons.

I should also mention that *Turandot* is set in China. This is important. So far in this book, a lot of our focus has been from the perspective of 'the West'. 'The West' is a quick way of describing the part of the world populated by mainly white people, that includes most of Europe and the USA. It might also include Australia, because a large chunk of the Australian population are descendants of people from Britain. The West isn't just a place. It's also a perspective, meaning that you can actually see the whole world from a Western point of view. This point of view sees Western culture (music, food, clothing, and so on) as *normal*, and non-Western culture as *different*.

Operas are generally seen as part of Western culture, but *Turandot* was about Eastern culture, written by an Italian composer. This means that it looks at Eastern culture (in this case Chinese culture) from a Western perspective.

Why is any of this important?

Well, one of the big risks of a single perspective is that it can be very limited. It can end up relying on stereotypes, creating unrealistic images of 'different' people from 'other' cultures. I put those words in inverted commas because no one is different and nothing is other. It all depends on where you're looking from.

Between the late 1880s and the early 1930s, there were dozens of very popular opera-style musicals with a Chinese theme. It was a trend that saw Asia as exciting and exotic. Another word for this is *fetishisation*, whereby a particular culture is seen as attractive because of its difference to whatever is seen as normal. These shows had titles such as *A Chinese Honeymoon*, *A Trip to Japan* and *Chu Chin Chow*, drawing audiences in on the idea that Asian culture was unusual, exciting and exotic. Over the years, *Turandot* has attracted some criticism because it includes offensive Chinese stereotypes, with characters called Ping, Pang and Pong, making fun of Chinese-sounding names.

It's worth saying that this book is very Western in its outlook. I have grown up in the West and my perspective centres Western culture. As we go further in our journey, keep an eye out for shifts in this perspective, and for non-Western influences on mainstream culture.

'Nessun Dorma' is a fascinating example of how art can celebrate one culture, while simultaneously pushing another culture to one side. It's all about power: who or what is in control, and how that world view remains dominant. On the one hand, it highlights Italian opera as powerful art for the whole world to enjoy, while quietly adding to the idea that the 'Far East' is interesting because it is different to what Europeans think is normal.

'Strange Fruit'

Billie Holiday (1939)

Question: When do we need music to help us to remember?

Sometimes the most powerful art comes from the darkest places. There's nothing nice about the story behind this song.

It starts with a picture from 1930. The picture is of an act of murder. The murder of two men, in a place called Indiana, in the USA. The two men are being hanged by the neck, in an awful type of murder known as lynching.

They are black. They are being killed because they are black. They are being killed because of racism.

It's a haunting, unbearable image, and one that no one should be forced to think about for too long. When a teacher from New York, USA, saw the picture, it haunted him. His name was Abel Meeropol and, like a lot of people living in the USA at the time, he believed in civil rights for black people.

Abel took all his feelings about the picture and turned them into a poem. The poem described the bodies of the black men as strange fruit, hanging from the trees, swinging in the breeze. The world 'strange' is important here, because it reminds us how unnatural this situation was, is and will always be. No one should die because of racism.

Eventually, the poem became a song, set to music. It was given new life and one of the people who heard it was a young jazz singer called Eleanora Fagan, who went by the name Billie Holiday. Billie had been singing in nightclubs since she was a teenager, touring all over America and helping to make jazz music popular.

'Strange Fruit' reminded Billie of her father, who had died when she was younger. Billie always felt as though her father had been denied the care he needed when he was ill, having been turned away from a hospital because he was black. This is the kind of pain and trauma that was common for black Americans at this time and would continue to exist deep into the twentieth century.

In this way, 'Strange Fruit' became a song of both personal and collective pain. It's a song that forces you to stop and realise the tragic waste of human life that comes with racism, making us look at the picture that we don't want to see. Keeping these images alive is important, not because it's a good thing to relive pain and trauma but because we shouldn't forget the crimes against humanity that have affected the global human family. This is why Billie Holiday decided to perform 'Strange Fruit' for years and years. Every time, she would sing it the same way: in total darkness apart from a spotlight on her face. Then, when it was over, the light would go out. When it came back on, Billie would be gone. And that was the end of the show.

It's a deeply affecting moment, to hear the pain in her voice, describing the ugliest extents of human cruelty.

Billie Holiday performed the song until she died at the age of only forty-four. In time, the song was adopted by civil rights activists as a symbol for change, while many people chose to look away. When Billie Holiday sang it, some audience members would applaud for minutes at a time, while some would walk out in silence. This is the reality of how different people deal with the harsh truths of injustice. Some of us face it head-on. Some of us choose to look away. Sometimes, like in the picture that inspired the poem that inspired the song 'Strange Fruit', some of us stand by while the injustice is happening, encouraging it to continue. That's what I haven't told you yet: that the picture is not simply of two dead men. It also shows a large crowd of onlookers, gathered to watch the lynchings, totally relaxed, comfortable, happy even, where racism had become so commonplace that it had actually become normal.

In any case, the victims of injustices often have no choice about how to respond at all. Victims are often silent, their voices taken away by the hatred of others. I won't let that happen here. Billie Holiday sang her song to remind the world that the victims of racist murder still mattered, and that they stay alive in our memories and our protest.

I will tell you now that those two murdered men had names: Thomas Shipp and Abram Smith – black men whose lives (and deaths) were little more than a sideshow for a shuffling crowd. Like you, I never knew these men, and neither did Billie Holiday, but their lives, cruelly extinguished in racist hate, have inspired music that asks us to remember.

'Black and White Rag'

Winifred Atwell (1952)

Question: When does a star become a superstar?

The first thing to say about Winifred Atwell is that she was a *huge* star. A superstar really, back in the 1950s, when popular music was still mainly heard on pianos played live in homes and public places. Winifred was a piano player herself. She was so good that she became famous, and her music was sold in the millions. In fact, she was the first black person to have a number one song in the UK music charts, and the first black artist to sell a million copies in the UK. At the peak of her fame, she could be seen driving around Brixton (where I would grow up decades later) in a shiny Rolls-Royce motor car (I can't afford one of those just yet). Eventually, she became so popular that she even ended up playing in private concerts for Queen Elizabeth II, and her hands were insured for £40,000. This meant that she was legally not allowed to do the washing up. For a black woman alive at a time when sexism and racism were commonplace, this is a truly amazing fact, reminding us of just how talented and respected Winifred was.

She was a skilled classical piano player. Having grown up in the Caribbean island of Trinidad, she went on to study in the USA before going to the Royal Academy of Music in the UK, one of the most famous colleges in the country, where she excelled.

Interestingly enough, it wasn't her classical playing that made her a star. There was another type of music that she had learned as a young pianist, called *ragtime*. The 'rag' in ragtime stands for 'raggedy'. It's a lively type of music that is full of notes being strung together in exciting rhythms, with the right hand doing all sorts of acrobatics at the top end of the keyboard. This makes it jumpy and fun. A similar type of music was *boogie-woogie*, which is as fun as the name sounds. A young Winifred first learned to play boogie-woogie after American soldiers in Trinidad said that she couldn't. Determined to prove them wrong, she went away and figured out how to play it herself, which she did very well.

Here, we can see styles of music that were treated very differently by mainstream music lovers coming together in one artist. Winifred Atwell took all the fun and liveliness of ragtime and played it with the skill of a classically trained expert pianist. When she performed live, she actually had two pianos: a beautiful grand piano that she would perform classical pieces on, and then her 'other' piano, a beat-up old junk shop upright piano that she would play her ragtime and boogie-woogie hits on.

'Black and White Rag' is much older than Winifred Atwell. It was written in 1908 by an American composer called George Botsford. When Winifred recorded her version in 1952, it started off a whole new trend for what was known as 'honky-tonk' piano. People fell in love with the ragtime style and, importantly, it was embraced by the British public. Shortly after 'Black and White Rag', fans of Winfred's piano were treated to 'Britannia Rag' (celebrating Britain) and 'Coronation Rag' (celebrating the new Queen). Winifred Atwell had successfully made a musical bridge between funky American piano and British society.

Winifred Atwell is a perfect example of just how big the musical world really is and just how complicated things can get when it comes to issues of power and identity. Her fame seemed to rise above the discrimination she would have faced as a black woman, but this might have been because she was accepted by mainstream society. This might prove the power of music to bridge huge gaps of racism, sexism and other forms of discrimination. Or it might prove that marginalised people have to go into unknown realms of success to be accepted. We can celebrate her success and the barriers she broke down as a pioneering artist, but her story is a reminder of how success can make it easier for things, and people, to be accepted.

Winifred Atwell transformed popular music in Britain, having been born in a country, Trinidad, that was under British rule when she was a child, and wouldn't be fully independent until 1962. When Queen Elizabeth was busy being raised as a princess in the palaces of England, did she have any idea that a young girl from Trinidad would one day be entertaining her with piano sounds that no one had heard before? I doubt it.

As we go forward in our musical journey we'll meet artists who broke barriers and hear songs that changed people's expectations of music. These are important moments. They expand the landscape and widen the horizons, making the world bigger than it was before, with new sounds from new places, making new links and pushing towards new futures.

'Hound Dog'

Big Mama Thornton (1953)

Question: How did black American culture travel through music?

By the time you got to the 1950s, the music industry was big, BIG business. You can even tell from the phrase 'music industry' that modern music has become a whole system of production as much as a way of creating art and celebrating life. As more and more ordinary people were buying music of their own, finding and recording 'hit' records promised glittering dreams and, if you were really lucky, massive financial wealth.

Like a lot of people, Sam Phillips was looking for a way to make his millions from the recording industry. As a young man growing up in 1950s USA, Sam had a deep love of American music. This included black American music that hadn't yet been picked up by the white American mainstream. One example was the blues, which Sam thought to be a powerful genre of music. He believed that it could invite people to think hard about life and understand their own troubles, hopefully helping them to heal.

There's a word to describe black people that has fallen out of fashion since the mid-twentieth century. The word is *Negro*, and it dates back to the 1440s, when Spanish and Portuguese travellers first encountered darker-skinned people from various parts of Africa. 'Negro' simply translates to 'black'. As time rolled on, it became a catch-all label for black people living in America. And remember, these communities were often the descendants of black Africans who had been brought to north America as enslaved peoples. This partly explains why black music of the twentieth century is so often associated with pain and struggle, alongside energy and life. Black Americans had been forced to push through all the barriers that racism had constructed, and not end up defeated by them.

From the 1920s onwards, black music had been sold as 'race' records, designed to appeal to black American audiences. Sam Phillips was white, but he knew that black music had a unique appeal. The blues was full of hurt, but powerful too, because it was all about how black people had to survive in a hostile world. This, more than anything, is something that people at the time would have called a 'Negro sound'.

Sam had an idea. He thought that if he could find a white singer with the 'Negro sound' he could make a lot of money. And it wasn't long until he found exactly what (or rather who) he was looking for, when a teenager called Elvis Presley turned up at his studios to record a couple of songs for his mother. Elvis Presley went on to become one of the biggest recording artists in all music history, drawing millions of fans and selling millions of records. He was young and vibrant, with a deep, crooning voice and exciting dance moves. Importantly, he also specialised in black music at a time when black musicians were not fully welcomed into the American mainstream.

One of Elvis Presley's biggest hits is a song called 'Hound Dog'. It's a funky, growling rock 'n' roll classic with machine gun drums and big, chunky guitars, with Elvis growling over the top. However, 'Hound Dog' was originally recorded in 1953 by a blues singer called Willie Mae Thornton with the nickname 'Big Mama'. Mae Thornton was black, and she was a woman. Her original version of the song has all the authority of someone with the nickname she had.

The fact that Big Mama Thornton was never as big a star as Elvis raises questions about racism in modern America. In the 1950s, the USA was definitely ready for black music, but wasn't quite ready for black superstars to take the glory.

It's important to remember here that music is for everybody. Sometimes, too often really, conversations about race and racism can start to feel like a see-saw, or a tug of war, whereby someone has to be the winner. Even worse, it can feel as though all white people are being blamed for all racism, at all times. It's not as simple as that. Racism isn't just when white people treat black people in a bad way: it's a whole complex system of power and inequality that reaches far back into history and spreads like gas throughout the air we breathe. This is how Big Mama Thornton could be a successful recording artist at a time when black Americans were still suffering racism, and have a song that wouldn't make it big until it was rerecorded by a white singer.

And it's a song that was written by two white songwriters called Jerry Leiber and Mike Stoller. Here, we're seeing an example of how black, female artists have made huge contributions to music history, but can still go unrecognised. Just over thirty years before Willie Mae Thornton recorded 'Hound Dog', a song called 'Crazy Blues' was recorded and released by a blues singer called Mamie Smith. It wasn't the first time this particular song was recorded, but Smith's version was the first song to become a blues hit, selling tens of thousands of copies in its first few weeks alone. After this song, the white American public became used to the idea of popular music by black artists.

As we go forward in our journey, keep an eye out for moments like this, when music that people haven't paid much attention to starts to become popular. These are important moments, because they are moments when things start to change. And if nothing else, this is a book about how music changes the world.

'The Twist'

Chubby Checker (1960)

Question: Can a dance move change society forever?

Very often, music is for dancing. This is the story of one of the most important dances of all time.

The dance is called 'the twist'. As a dance move, it's quite simple. You bend your arms at the elbow and put your fists by your sides, then you twizzle your hips left to right, while grinding your feet into the floor at the same time, as though you're trying to dig a hole into the ground with only your legs to help you. Chubby Checker, real name Ernest Evans, described it as 'wiping your bottom with an invisible towel'. As you can tell, the twist is a lot of fun, and in the early 1960s it became a huge dance craze that swept all across the world.

It started off in the USA, when Chubby Checker released a song called 'The Twist' in 1960. The song was originally recorded in 1958 by a group called Hank Ballard and the Midnighters, but it didn't become really popular until Chubby Checker's version. As a song, 'The Twist' is all about dancing, calling you to the dance floor from the very first line, asking everyone to come on, baby, and do the twist.

Within months, Chubby Checker's song had made the jump across the Atlantic Ocean to the UK, where young teenagers started twisting like mad. Dance venues across the country started featuring special rock 'n' roll 'twist nights', where British people came together to enjoy black American music and try out the latest new dance move at the same time.

All of this is very exciting, but what makes the twist an important piece of social history is how it was received by many adults in charge of the world at the time. Some of them were worried, or even scared of this new dance. Why? What could be so terrifying about twisting your hips and wiping your bum with an imaginary towel?

To answer this question, we have to start by remembering that in the early 1960s, rock 'n' roll was still new and exciting. This was a genre of music that no one had seen or heard before, full of raw energy and the kind of adolescent excitement that makes some adults very worried indeed. Rock 'n' roll has always been seen as a sexual kind of music, and many adults are absolutely terrified of young people being exposed to anything sexual at all. So when this dance came along, with its instructions to twist at the hip, there was a bit of sexual danger that made many people think twice.

In the UK, the twist actually drew complaints from all over the country. It sounds unbelievable, but people even contacted the BBC to say that they didn't like the way this new dance made young people act. But really, I think that the main reason that the twist wasn't trusted was because it was about to change things, forever.

See, the thing about the twist as a dance is that you can do it alone. In fact, you can do it alone or in groups. Side by side, crowded together, in your own space, with anyone else or not. This concept was mind-blowing. Up until this point, dancing was always seen as an activity for a *couple*, specifically two people, one male, one female. This rule had existed in the UK, Europe and the West for centuries. It's a history that might go as far back as Germany in the fourteenth century or earlier, where trends first emerged of boy/girl dancing couples. Soon, it became a social norm for male and female partners to dance together with strict rules about how to move and where to go. These dances had specific sequences that you had to follow, and if you got it wrong, you were breaking all the rules.

Skip forward a few hundred years and 'The Twist' brought about a new era of liberation, or freedom, on the dance floors of the modern West. And this meant a relaxing of the kind of rules that were always intended to keep people in their place. Suddenly, girls could dance with girls, boys could dance with boys, anyone could dance with anyone, doing moves that hinted at something sexual at the same time. Phew. It was a revolution in music.

This is the first time that we've mentioned sexuality in this book. It's a theme that will come up again as we go further on our musical journey, exploring how Western society has feared homosexuality and struggled to accept gay people. 'The Twist' is an example of how music can help bring about social and political change, even if it isn't intended to be political in the first place. 'The Twist' is all about fun and freedom, but in a world where not everyone is equally free, that in itself can actually become a political thing.

'Ue o Muite Arukō'

Kyu Sakamoto (1961)

Question: How do you turn sadness into celebration?

You've had enough.

You don't want the country you live in to be locked into a military pact with a country it recently fought with. You disagree with this plan. You don't want foreign military bases to be set up in the country you call home.

So you take to the streets.

You go to a protest. You join hundreds of thousands of other young people in the streets, to show how strongly you feel. The protests are huge, taking place all over the country.

But they don't work.

The government doesn't listen. Nothing changes. And you go home, trying not to feel crushed by the weight of failure.

In 1960, this is the situation that a songwriter called Rokusuke Ei found himself in. He had taken part in protests against a security treaty between Japan and the USA that allowed the presence of US military bases in Japan. Like thousands of others, Rokusuke didn't want to be in a situation where Japan could be brought into dangerous international conflicts.

The lyrics to 'Ue o Muite Arukō' tell the story of a person who is whistling and looking upwards while walking, to stop themselves from crying. This is basically what happened to Rokusuke after the protest. These are words of dejection and frustration, realising that you haven't got the power to change forces beyond your control.

The song doesn't sound depressing, though. Performed by Japanese singer Kyu Sakamoto, it sounds almost optimistic, maybe even *happy*, though tinged with a slight sadness. The lyrics make no reference to protest or politics, instead talking about general feelings of loss and love – perfect for a pop song.

And this is exactly what happened. 'Ue o Muite Arukō' became a hit song. It soon became number one in six different countries and has sold 13 million copies, making it one of the best-selling singles of all time.

For a song that was sung in Japanese, this was very important. At this point in our story the world is a very separated place. Countries in the West, that spoke English, were not quick to accept non-Western cultures. In the US, 'Ue o Muite Arukō' was the first song by an Asian artist to reach number one in the Hot 100 charts, and it won't be until 2020 that we see another. Historically, the West has seen the East as somewhere far away and exotic. The Second World War had seen the USA fight against Japan, which contributed to lots of racism against Japanese people.

Conflicts between East and West can be seen in the fact that in 1963, 'Ue o Muite Arukō' was given another title in Western countries: 'Sukiyaki'. *Sukiyaki* is the name of a Japanese type of food, cooked with beef. This has absolutely nothing to do with the original song, its lyrics or the protests that inspired it. The name was chosen because it was thought to be easier for English-speaking people to say, and was recognisable for white Westerners who knew little of Japanese culture. In a sense, this might be seen as offensive – repackaging a Japanese song for the ease of a non-Japanese audience.

We've already seen the stereotyping of Asian cultures back in the 1920s, part of a legacy of racism towards Asia that exists in Western culture. In a way, this particular song is another reminder in this book of the power of politics. In the 1960s, Japan was beginning to re-establish itself after the Second World War. In a way, the Western world was ready to accept Japanese culture, and the countries who had been at conflict were in need of a fresh start. The lyrics to 'Ue o Muite Arukō' speak to this optimism, with reference to looking up, looking forward and seeing good fortune in the future. The title in full Japanese is 上を向いて歩こう, which translates to 'I Look Up as I Walk.'

After 'Ue o Muite Arukō' was first recorded, a number of other versions have been made. My favourite of these stories is from the group A Taste of Honey, in 1981. One of the group's singers (called Janice-Marie Johnson) had first heard the song as a child and, without knowing what any of the Japanese words meant, learned it all by heart. Years later, as an adult in 1981, she recorded a new version of 'Sukiyaki' and it became one of the group's biggest songs. Even better, Janice-Marie had surprised many people by choosing to record a Japanese song as a black artist – even though music has no borders at all.

The musical world is a world full of surprises. Here, we have a song that began with anger about military cooperation between USA and Japan, that ended with a musical collaboration between those same countries, twenty years apart. This, I think, is part of the progress that the world was making – if not solving problems of power and conflict, at least pushing towards a new climate of hope, cooperation and cultures being shared.

'A Change Is Gonna Come'

Sam Cooke (1964)

Question: When does music become a force for change?

The history of the USA is full of conflict and struggles around race and racism. Going back as far as the birth of the country itself, the USA has wrestled with the fact that black, enslaved people have lived on the same soil as the white Americans who often owned them. It makes the name of the country itself quite ironic (the *United* States) when there has been so much division rather than unity.

Unlike slaveowners in the UK, whose slaves worked far away in Caribbean islands like Jamaica and Barbados, slaveowners in the US lived in the same country as their slaves. This meant that they felt the need to control black people who lived with them, even after the slave trade was abolished in the USA, in 1865, following a violent civil war within the country.

It was never going to be a simple transition into a racism-free world. After 1865, slavery continued illegally for many decades. Meanwhile, the laws of the land were violently racist against black Americans. In some southern states, laws were passed that made it illegal for black and white people to mix, or integrate. These laws of segregation meant that black Americans were denied rights enjoyed by white people, with serious restrictions on their freedom too. These laws became known as the 'Jim Crow' laws (referring to a song and dance used to poke fun at black people).

Discrimination against black people remained common across the USA. Efforts were made to prevent black Americans from voting, and the legal system was manipulated in a way that meant that black people could be made to work for free, like slaves. To this day, the USA has nearly five times more black people in prison compared to white people. This is a situation that has been encouraged by a combination of economic poverty, unfair sentencing rules and a police force with a history of targeting black communities. These mainly black prisoners get paid very little for hours of physical labour, doing work that big companies make profit from. So, yes, in a sense, a type of slavery is still happening in modern America.

Let's go back a step. The Jim Crow era was met with protest from people who wanted equality. These kinds of protests had happened before, but as we moved into the twentieth century, a new civil rights movement began to grow. Efforts were being made by black Americans (or African Americans) to gain the rights they had been denied. There was also a need to push back against the threat of racist groups such as the Ku Klux Klan, a group formed in 1865, whose members believed in white supremacy and murdered black people in horrific acts of terrorism.

By the 1960s, there had been a number of highlight moments in civil rights history. 1954 saw the US Supreme Court rule that segregation could never be equal, following a huge case where a black man called Oliver Brown fought to send his child to a white school. A year later, a woman called Rosa Parks refused to give her seat on a bus to a white passenger, an act of protest that led to a boycott of buses in Montgomery, Alabama. Two years after that in 1957, nine black students attended a white school in a place called Little Rock. It was such a risky thing to do that they needed military protection. Soon, a whole series of civil rights marches and protests were taking place, giving fresh momentum to the cause. And then in 1963 a quarter of a million people marched to Washington, DC, the home of the US government, to hear Martin Luther King give his legendary 'I Have a Dream' speech. It felt like change was on the way.

The civil rights movement came with a soundtrack, and that sound was the sound of *soul*. Soul music came from the black experience. It was deep and serious and beautiful in its emotional honesty. It felt real, more real than flimsy pop music designed to only make you dance. Soul made you think, but even more, it made you feel. Soul music was about pride and pain. Since the 1950s, it had grown more and more popular, so much so that white audiences were listening. But it spoke to black Americans in a deeper way.

The song 'A Change Is Gonna Come' sounds like a cry of hope. Its long, yearning notes stretch into the future, calling for a change that black Americans had been waiting decades for. It has painful strings, pounding drums and a sad-sounding French horn, every instrument adding to the reflective tone of the song. The singer, Sam Cooke, wrote the song about his experiences of discrimination and racism. He was partly inspired by a song from 1963 called 'Blowin' in the Wind' by a white folk artist called Bob Dylan. Bob's song asked simple, poetic questions about the world and how we treat each other. Then, when Sam heard Martin Luther King speak in 1963, he knew he had to write a protest song of his own.

A year after 'A Change Is Gonna Come' was released, white supremacists set off a bomb in a black church in the southern state of Alabama. Among those killed were four children. The bombers were part of the Ku Klux Klan and the attack was racially motivated. This is the reality of the civil rights struggle – lives were being lost while people were desperate for change.

Racism was never going to be solved by a single song, but big changes did eventually come. By the end of the 1960s, segregation had been made illegal and efforts were being made to legally stop racist discrimination in different parts of society, offering hope for a new, modern America.

'A Change Is Gonna Come' wasn't the first and won't be the last protest song in US history. As recently as

2015, a song called 'Alright' by a young rapper called Kendrick Lamar became an anthem for the Black Lives Matter movement, decades after Sam Cooke first sang for change in the 1960s.

Sam Cooke's song has become a permanent musical symbol of civil rights activism, and despite the many setbacks this fight has had, it remains as powerful now as it was then.

'Respect'

Aretha Franklin (1967)

Question: What does respect actually sound like?

There's a moment towards the end of 'Respect' where everything stops, the instruments take a brief pause, and Aretha Franklin spells out the word *respect*, one letter at a time.

R-E-S-P-E-C-T

It's a powerful moment in a powerful song, where the singer forces us to slow down and really think about that one word. *Respect*. It's something we all want, something we all need. The respect of other people, to be treated as a human being with the same rights as everybody else.

When Aretha sings this part, you can hear the determination in her voice. She wants to find out what respect means for her – what it would look like if she actually had the respect she knows she deserves. She is making a call for her rights, and demanding that her rights be respected.

There's a lot of royalty in modern music. Elvis Presley is known as 'the King of Rock 'n' Roll', Michael Jackson 'the King of Pop', even an artist famously known as *Prince*. Aretha Franklin is widely known as the 'Queen of Soul', a title that she earned through her incredible vocal performances. From a young age, Aretha Franklin was an impressive singer, able to bring songs to life with passion and emotion. It's something she developed in the church, her father having been a famous pastor with a powerful singing voice too.

Soul music has a lot to do with suffering. Black Americans in the 1960s were still living through an era of extreme racism, segregated from white Americans and denied basic human rights. The civil rights movement was all about this struggle. It was a sustained attempt by black Americans to win the respect that racism had taken away. Remember, many modern black Americans are the direct descendants of enslaved people who were transported from parts of Africa in the eighteenth century. These 'African Americans' were technically free from slavery, but they weren't really free at all. They weren't allowed to share spaces with white Americans. They were treated with contempt by the authorities. They were forced to live in deprived conditions. They were even targeted and physically attacked by ordinary people. At its worst, racism saw many black Americans become the victims of horrific murders, including cruel acts of *lynching* – for everyone to see.

In the truest sense of the word, they were completely, utterly *disrespected*.

Sam Cooke had already asked deep questions about when this dire situation would change back in 1964, offering a poignant new soundtrack to the civil rights movement. As a black *woman*, Aretha Franklin brought another important dimension to the mix. 'Respect' was originally written by a famous soul singer called Otis Redding in 1965. In the two years that followed, Aretha Franklin turned 'Respect' into her own song, singing it live onstage. She wasn't really asking for respect so much as stating that she already deserved it.

Here, we can start to see feminist ideas unfurl into

wider society. 'Respect' is full of life and energy, with big blaring horns and upbeat backing vocals, all fronted by one of the most famous voices in music history. It sounds obvious, almost silly to say out loud, but women and girls deserve the same respect as men and boys. However, societies all over the world have suffered from sexism for so long that women and girls are not treated equally. This was the case in the 1960s and, tragically, this is still the case today. The spirit of popular figures such as Aretha Franklin will remain an inspiration for female empowerment all over the world.

The 1960s saw a huge surge of feminism that really began to help people move towards gender equality in the modern world. The first wave had come in the early twentieth century and was largely focused on women's right to vote on political issues. This 'second wave', as it would come to be known, sparked something new. One big moment was the publication of book called *The Feminine Mystique* by Betty Friedan, who argued that modern women had been manipulated into a lifestyle that limited their potential. Another big moment was the formation of NOW (the National Organization for Women) in 1966. I would argue that 'Respect' by Aretha Franklin was a third big moment in this story, particularly for women of colour (as black women would have been called at the time).

In America, black women had a different set of experiences to their white peers, having to face the sting of racism as well as sexism. In the decades after Aretha Franklin first asked us to find out what R-E-S-P-E-C-T meant for her (as a black woman), black feminism became more and more prominent. By the time you got to the 1970s, a whole new idea called 'womanism' had come about, led by the work of a writer called Alice Walker and focusing carefully on the lives of black women. One of Alice Walker's most famous books, *The Color Purple*, is all about black women finding strength in each other in a sexist and racist world. One of the main characters, Shug Avery, is a confident singer who commands respect from everyone.

When Aretha Franklin died in in 2018, there was an outpouring of praise for her life and legacy. A whole line-up of black American artists, both male and female, paid tribute to her life. Only a year earlier, her activism against injustice meant that she refused to sing at the inauguration of Donald Trump. She didn't respect his presidency enough, so she made a stand against it.

Until we have equality and fairness, the fight for equality will never end. As someone who lived through unfairness and inequality, Aretha Franklin knew all about what it meant to win the respect you deserve, and continues to inspire the world to give respect wherever it is due.

'What's Going On'

Marvin Gaye (1971)

Question: Really, what is going on?

In 1971, Marvin Gaye had lots of questions to ask of the world around him:

Why is there so much fighting? Why are mothers crying? Why are the streets full of people protesting? Where is all this anger coming from? Why are people dying, in wars that don't seem to make any sense at all? Why so much hatred, when there should be love? What's going on?

It's a good question. In 1971, the USA was involved in military conflict in Vietnam that had gone back to the 1960s. It was a violent time, with bombings and battles that killed thousands. The Vietnam War led to more than half a million US soldiers being placed in Vietnam, fighting against groups from North Vietnam who believed in communism. At this time, the world was locked into global arguments over what was better: communism (where a country's resources would be owned by the government and shared out according on need), or capitalism (where individuals can get as much private wealth as they want). The USA was against the spread of communism and had a government willing to fight against it, all over the world.

Many American people were against the war. They staged protests all over the US, calling for the government to withdraw from the conflict and hopefully save the lives of soldiers and civilians who were being killed in violent attacks. A US strategy of bombing North Vietnamese soldiers from the air led to the deaths of many innocent people. The US also used chemical weapons: jellied petrol (called napalm) which would burn and stick to the skin, and high strength weedkiller (called 'Agent Orange') which would destroy crops and green areas that Vietnamese fighters could hide in.

These weapons did horrendous damage to Vietnam and its citizens, encouraging many people to go against the war overall.

Protests against the Vietnam War were met with opposition from the government itself, leading to social unrest. By the end of the 1960s, the USA started to withdraw troops from Vietnam, but the conflict was not over. Hundreds of thousands of people had been killed, and US air strikes would happen again.

It's in this situation that Marvin Gaye was writing a new album, in 1970. The album, called *What's Going On*, is written from the perspective of a veteran US soldier returning home from the Vietnam War. Marvin Gaye did not fight in the war, but he had seen young men being sent away to fight and anti-war protesters being attacked by the police. He also had a brother who had been a soldier in Vietnam, who he shared letters with about what it was like to be part of all that trauma.

The song 'What's Going On' itself was originally written by Renaldo Benson, a friend of Marvin's who was in a band called the Four Tops. Renaldo said that the song was not actually a protest song, but a love song that was asking what was happening in the world and calling out for less hatred, more love.

'What's Going On' sounds like a search for answers.

It's slow and soulful, with low wailing horns that drift. It's easy to listen to, even though it asks the most difficult questions. And in 1971 it joined a collection of songs that were protesting against the violence and suffering in that was happening in Vietnam. Next, we shall hear a song that offers something like an answer to Marvin Gaye's question, but (in our very broken world) it's a task that isn't always easy to do . . .

'Imagine'

John Lennon (1971)

Question: Can we imagine a whole new world, through song?

The idea of a war is too big to hold in your head.

It's so big that most of us don't spend any real time thinking about it.

It's too awful, with too much suffering. To really think that violence between groups of people can become so extreme that it can lead to the destruction of homes and the deaths of hundreds, thousands, millions. Even writing these words, I can't comprehend what that would feel like.

And yet, wars are common. You've probably studied some of them at school, the 'world wars' in particular. You probably know something about the First and Second World Wars that took place in the twentieth century, long before most of us were even born.

I was born in 1982 and luckily, I've never experienced war up close, having lived in peaceful places since I was born. But in the four decades that span my life so far, there has been some sort of major conflict going on in the world, somewhere, at all times.

So really, have I actually lived during peaceful times at all? Have any of us? This is the problem: that the world is set up in a way that makes it easy to look away, if the problems seem far, far away or the people involved seem different to us. When we don't think about the experiences of people who are suffering, it can feel like that suffering doesn't exist.

It's not about feeling guilty. It's about stopping to think about the reality of the situation, because the world we live in is a flawed one, full of suffering that should be avoidable. These stories are difficult, but we have to acknowledge them if we have any chance of imagining something better.

This is what 'Imagine' is all about. It's a song where John Lennon asks us to, well, imagine – a different world. A world without possessions, money, religions or countries: things that people care deeply about that we often end up disagreeing about and fighting over.

It says a lot that 'Imagine' is the most successful song of John Lennon's solo career. (He wrote it with his wife, a woman called Yoko Ono, who hasn't been given the credit for writing what is one of the most famous songs of all time.) Since it was first written, 'Imagine' has been performed by hundreds of artists all over the world and continues to be sung today whenever people want to think about peace. It shows us that people have a desire for peace and unity, yes, but it also shows that people are more willing to accept the idea of peace rather than work towards the difficult process of making it really happen. We also need to remember that John Lennon was asking us to imagine a world with no possessions from the position of being an unbelievably wealthy rock star. It might be more useful to find out what life is like for the many millions who don't have as many possessions as they need, before working out how to improve the situation.

When you really think about it, 'Imagine' opens up an important debate about the role of creative people in our troubled world. John Lennon was not a politician, or a business leader, or the head of a school or anything like that. He was a songwriter from Liverpool in the UK, who was inspired by music from black America to make music with his friends. Creative people have one job to do – to make art. And creativity is the solution to every human problem. Science is creative. Technology is creative. Food production, politics, education, it all needs the ability to dream of something that doesn't yet exist. Humans have evolved into the cleverest species on this planet precisely because we can do this. We can imagine.

It might not be too weird to argue that artistic people offer the world something just as important as big businesses and governments. They don't offer plans and solutions and strategies for the future: they offer a way of understanding the world, reflecting it back to us through art that we can enjoy. Many artists say that they feel a responsibility to offer the truth, through their visions. This, I think, is why stories, films and music (creative things) are so popular. Humans find hope and understanding, and truth, in art.

In 1980, John Lennon was shot and killed in New York City. He was killed by one of his fans, a twenty-five-year-old man who later said that he was angry about the fact that John Lennon had such a rich lifestyle. The man who killed John Lennon got close to him by asking him for an autograph, which John was happy to provide. This was a senseless murder that caused great pain across the world. On 14 December 1980, millions of people observed a ten-minute silence in memory of John Lennon, as invited by his wife, Yoko Ono. John would be remembered as a man who made contributions to music, art and peace.

In 'Imagine', John says that he might be a *dreamer*. Then he says that he's not the only one, before ending with the idea that one day the world will feel like one place. When you think about everything I've written in this chapter, that's a very big dream indeed. It's a simple idea and a simple song. We should remember that many millions of people have died in senseless acts of violence, but unlike John Lennon, their names are not remembered. More than fifty years after 'Imagine' was written, we're still having to imagine a world of peace where everyone is truly united . . .

. . . in perfect harmony.

'I'd Like to Teach the World to Sing (In Perfect Harmony)'

Hillside Singers (1971)

Question: Can you sell a dream?

This might sound like the perfect follow-on from all that dreaming we heard about in the last chapter, but the musical world isn't always a simple place. Let's talk business.

The Coca-Cola company. It's one of the biggest companies in the world. So big that I'm certain you have already heard of it (and probably drunk its product).

A version of the song 'I'd Like to Teach the World to Sing (In Perfect Harmony)' was originally used in a television advert for Coca-Cola in 1971. It's a simple advert, starting with a single voice singing. Then the camera zooms out and you see lots of other people who are also singing, on a green hilltop. The people are all different, seemingly from different countries and cultures with different shades of skin, but they are all enjoying a bottle of Coke. Then at the end, a message on the screen tells you that these people were brought together from all over the world to share this special moment.

The advert is designed to make you feel united with other people. And, like the song says, it invites you to link Coca-Cola, the real thing, with our real feelings of unity.

The first line of the song is happy and welcoming, talking about buying a home for the world.

Buying. It's an interesting word. Not *offering* the world a home, or *giving* the world a home, but *buying* the world a home. And then a few moments later, the song talks about *buying* the world a Coke.

In the full lyrics to the song, not used in the advert,

there's no mention of buying anything at all. The song talks about building the world a home, seeing everyone holding hands and teaching the world to sing in peace and love.

We have to remember what I said at the start of this chapter – that Coca-Cola is a business. The whole point of a business is to provide a product or service that makes money for the people who own that business. This idea is at the core of something called *capitalism*, which is a huge part of the human global story. Capitalism is all about money – buying and selling things for profit. Currently, most of the world runs along capitalist lines because having money is an idea that everyone easily understands.

In capitalism, products and services are owned and controlled by people, for profit, rather than by the government. One alternative to capitalism is *socialism*, where the production of goods and services is owned by the state. But money (no matter which system it exists in) comes with greed and poverty, whereby wealth is not shared equally among those who need it. Right now, the world is full of people who have too much money and people who don't have enough money.

Later in this book, we'll see how disagreements over how to live have led to major political problems and even conflict between different countries. In the history of people, *how* we live very often becomes a reason for *why* we fight.

Coca-Cola was originally created in the USA in 1886 and has since become available all over the world. During the Second World War, bottling factories were set up around the world, which helped spread the taste of Coke to non-Americans. Politically, Coca-Cola can be seen as a symbol of capitalism. Over the years, countries who have disagreed with the USA (and its approach to politics) have expressed their disagreement in different ways, sometimes banning the production or sale of Coca-Cola, or encouraging people not to drink it. For example:

- Until 1994, Coca-Cola was banned in Vietnam as a result of trade restrictions linked to the war between the USA and Vietnam.
- In Thailand in 2003, protesters against the invasion of Iraq (led by the USA) poured Coca-Cola into the streets as a symbol.
- Up until 2012, all US companies including Coca-Cola were banned in Myanmar, south-east Asia.

Right now, there are two countries where Coca-Cola cannot be bought or sold: Cuba (where production stopped after a communist revolution in 1962) and North Korea (where the product has been banned since the war between Korea and USA in the 1950s).

In 1971, 60 per cent of Americans said they were against the war in Vietnam, while a war between India and Pakistan threatened horrific violence. Elsewhere, a *coup d'état* in Uganda led to the regime of a leader called Idi Amin, who would become one of the most brutal dictators in world history. In the UK, a bomb attack took place at the UK's then tallest building, the Post Office Tower in London (also known as the BT Tower). These are just some examples of how the world lacked harmony when 'I'd Like to Teach the World to Sing (In Perfect Harmony)' was first released.

The Hillside Singers sang of peace and love in a world that is not always peaceful or loving, and their song was used by one of the biggest companies in history to sell drinks. And here's something that might shock you, or not: The group was actually put together by an advertising company in the first place . . . Which means that the song was always about making money.

Or was it?

In life, you can choose to be cynical (questioning

everything) or idealistic (with positive hopes). Is this advert 'the real thing' or just a way of selling cola? Should we celebrate the vision Coca-Cola created in this advert, or think about the realities of conflicts that were taking place at the time? Bill Backer, the advertising executive behind the Hillside Singers, said that he saw Coca-Cola as 'a tiny bit of commonality between all peoples . . . that can bring people together'. Fifty-one years later, in 2022, it was announced that a famous fashion model called Kate Moss was to be the creative director for the Diet Coke brand. One of her aims was to somehow use Diet Coke to 'inspire generations', something that Bill Backer tried to do with the song in this chapter.

It's impossible to know how much he was motivated by this idea, rather than making lots of profit, but maybe the idea of being together, in harmony, is the goal we should always be looking towards – whether we have a fizzy drink or not.

'Rocket Man (I Think It's Going to Be a Long, Long Time)'

Elton John (1972)

Question: Why do we struggle to embrace the future?

Here are three facts about space travel and the year 1972:

- By 1972, probes launched from the planet Earth had successfully landed on both Venus and Mars.
- In 1972, it had been three years since the first humans had walked on the Moon.
- Five years after 1972, the USA would send two probes named *Voyager* into space, seeking to explore the gas giant planets of the outer solar system.

Here are three facts about the *Voyager* probes:

- Each *Voyager* probe carried with it a golden record.
- The records contain sounds and images that reveal some of the sounds and sights of planet Earth, including greetings in fifty-five languages and music from all over the world.
- One of the songs featured on the *Voyager* gold disc is the rock 'n' roll classic 'Johnny B. Goode' by Chuck Berry.

Here are three facts about the artist known as Elton John:

- Elton John is one of the most famous rock 'n' roll artists of the twentieth century, with more than 300 million records sold during his career.
- In 1979, Elton John released his very own version of 'Johnny B. Goode'.
- Elton John said in an interview from 1992 that he is 'quite comfortable about being gay'.

Here are three facts about being gay:

- The American Psychiatric Association listed homosexuality as 'psychiatric disorder' until 1973.
- Same-sex activity was illegal in England and Wales until 1967.
- The fight for LGBTQ+ (lesbian, gay, bisexual, transgender, queer and all other sexual identities) rights has continued in countries all over the world for numerous decades. As it stands, you might be legally allowed to have a same-sex marriage or you might face the death penalty, depending on which country you are in.

So why did I choose to put all of this together?

Well, I find it fascinating, and infuriating, that while humans can be seeking to map out the mysteries of space and the universe, we can at the same time be struggling to accept something as simple as love. The 1970s marked a huge moment of progress for our species, sending out probes on rockets that would leave clues for alien life about who we are and what we do. Right now, in 2023, the *Voyager* probes are still sending information back to Earth, travelling at thousands of miles an hour. Who knows? In centuries' time, distant life forms may well discover the golden discs, work out how to play them, and hear our sounds from the ancient past. It's a humbling thought.

And yet, here we are in the late twentieth century, with people still being persecuted for the simple fact of being gay. How can we be so advanced and so backwards at the same time? It's maddening.

'Rocket Man' comes with the subtitle 'I Think It's Going to Be a Long, Long Time'. Written by Bernie Taupin, it tells the story of an astronaut going to Mars, wondering when he'll ever return home. It's a hopeful but sad-sounding song, with strained, longing vocals over a thoughtful, reaching piano. It talks about missing the Earth and missing your loved ones. When Elton sings that he's not the man they think he is at all, it sounds defiant too. Add it all up and it sounds a lot like humans, alone in space, reaching out for big things that we can't fully understand.

And yet, so much of what we try to understand can be found in music. Back when Elton John was Reginald Dwight, before he changed his name, he found a way of expressing himself through music and the piano. Music allowed him to communicate himself to the world when things felt restrictive and limited. When he was a young man, just out of school, his father tried to encourage him away from music in favour of a more traditional career, like working in a bank. This was part of the reason that Elton chose to wear flamboyant, outrageous outfits onstage – he was letting go and being free. As a child, young Reginald had grown up listening to piano players like Winifred Atwell (who we met on page 37). Her energetic, exciting style influenced him directly, especially the joy with which she would turn and grin at her audience while playing – something that Elton John would do too in his famous live performances.

In 1990, two years before the Elton John interview mentioned earlier, *Voyager 1* took a photograph of Earth from about six billion kilometres away. From this incredible distance, Earth is little more than a pixel, a tiny, pale blue dot on a backdrop of endless . . . space. It's a powerful image, reminding us of how small we are and how all we have, while we're here, is each other. When you think about it like that, the thought of hating people for who they are and what they do becomes ludicrous.

To me, 'Rocket Man' is like a soundtrack of hope and yearning. Keep reading; this isn't the last time we'll see Elton John in these pages and it isn't the last time that we'll think about LGBTQ+ rights, as well as the rights of all people. As the writer Carl Sagan said in 1994, we have a 'responsibility to deal more kindly with one another, and to preserve and cherish the pale blue dot, the only home we've ever known'.

Exactly.

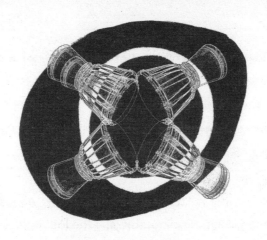

'Zombie'

Fela Kuti (1977)

Question: What does protest sound like?

Sometimes, you have to stand up and fight. Not necessarily physically, with your hands and feet, but against an idea or things that you believe to be wrong.

Some of the biggest fights you can have in the world are political – where you disagree with the way things are run or controlled by dominant groups. In fact, it's fair to say that many conflicts in human history (and in this book) are political in nature.

Music can be a big part of a political fight. It can be a way of saying what you disagree with, or shouting about what makes you unhappy. It can be a protest too, as we have seen with songs like 'Respect' and 'A Change Is Gonna Come', and as we shall see again soon.

We're now in Nigeria, part of a very modern Africa. In 1977, Olufela Ransome-Kuti was well on his way to becoming a huge superstar in African music. Since the 1960s, he had developed a new style of music called Afrobeat, which combined traditional African highlife with funk and jazz from the USA with salsa from South America and calypso from the Caribbean. Having spent time in America, Fela had also been influenced by the Black Panthers, a political group of social activists who believed in getting rights for all black people. The 'Black Power' movement became a big part of Fela's mission in music. He even decided to drop the 'Ransome' part of his name, which he believed to be a slave name, not linked to his Nigerian heritage.

Under his new name, Fela Kuti set about making exciting new music with his band, Africa 70. The music they made was energetic and funky, full of horns and drums and rhythms from all over the world. Fela deliberately sang his lyrics in a dialect called 'pidgin' – a type of English that could be understood by different communities all over the African continent. The point was simple: Fela wanted his music to be heard and understood by as many Africans as possible, even if they spoke hundreds of different languages.

Fela Kuti had something to say, and this is where the song 'Zombie' comes into play. A zombie is an unthinking being, a mindless creature that can't feel anything and does whatever it has been programmed to do. With his song, Fela Kuti was accusing the soldiers of the Nigerian army of acting like zombies, just blindly carrying out their orders as given by the government. In particular, Fela did not agree with the violence used by the army.

'Zombie' was a huge hit among Nigerian people. At over twelve minutes long, it's a whole musical journey in itself, finding grooves and rhythms for the instrumentalists to play with, with pulsing drums and horns that seem to speak to each other in some non-verbal, excited language. It contains big crashing drums and the more expressive 'talking drums' that originate from west Africa. Traditionally, these drums have been used in countries such as Nigeria and Ghana to send messages between different villages, communicating through the warping sounds of drums pulled by strings.

It wasn't long after the release of 'Zombie' that tensions between Fela Kuti and the government bubbled over into a tragic, violent conclusion. It is thought that over one thousand members of the military gathered to storm into Fela's home, a commune called Kalakuta Republic. Fela was physically beaten and his mother, who lived with him, died after being thrown from a window. After destroying Fela's music studio, the troops burned his commune down.

What we can we learn from 'Zombie'? Is it that the governments can be incredibly dangerous when they are challenged and opposed? Is it that conflict will always lead to more conflict? Perhaps a terrible reminder that the world can too easily lean towards chaos when people find themselves in disagreement.

Fela's music is part of a legacy of resistance and opposition that makes him one of the most famous musicians in African history. His music sounds as urgent today as it did in the 1970s; music that was deliberately trying to bring about change. He remains a controversial figure (well known for speaking out and upsetting the authorities), but his aim was always to speak out against things that he thought were unfair. The fact that he used music to be heard, and to unite people against injustice, is a reminder of the power of music to say things that you might be afraid to say. It's not just about having a good time or starting a party; music can scare the people in charge, and it can equally bring about meaningful change.

'Trans-Europe Express'

Kraftwerk (1977)

Question: Can you hear the future?

One of the most powerful things that humans do is dream of the future. We do it in our stories, our inventions, our hopes and our art. We visualise what might be, and if we work at it, these visions can become reality.

It's how every invention begins – as an idea. Something futuristic that isn't possible yet.

A lot of music is *not* futuristic. Music can be traditional, using instruments that already exist to create sounds that we already understand. There's nothing wrong with this. This is simply how we share culture and make connections with history, in order to better understand ourselves.

But sometimes, music is all about pushing the boundaries. This can be incredibly exciting, when new ideas come with new sounds. This is often through new technology that no one has ever used before. Think about it – how every single musical instrument had to be invented at some point in history, by someone with a new idea. And how these inventions can change the face of music forever.

Kraftwerk definitely dreamed of the future. It's the name of a band from Germany who came together in 1969, led by Ralf Hütter and Florian Schneider. The name Kraftwerk translates as 'power station', which gives you a good idea of what their musical style is all about: it's powerful and electric. It relates to the city of Dusseldorf, which is famous for its industrial growth and dense network of motorways, known in Germany as *autobahns*. *Autobahn* was even the name of Kraftwerk's fourth album, released in 1974.

Kraftwerk very quickly became pioneers in

electronic music. Their songs were full of new, experimental electronic instruments and sounded like robots were making the music, rather than people. The sounds they created didn't seem human at all, with synthesizers, electronic drums and vocoders that made normal voices sound like machines. They even invented totally new instruments to create sounds that never existed.

'Trans-Europe Express' is the perfect example of how electronic music could feel alive and robotic at the same time. It pulses on an endless electronic drum, with haunting synthesized strings and sparse vocals. This was a totally new soundtrack to a world that was rebuilding itself after the Second World War, the biggest war ever seen. Humanity had to look to the future after having experienced the senseless violence of a world war. And as a country which had been defeated, Germany was in the process of paving a new future, having been split into East Germany and West Germany in 1949. Dusseldorf (where the members of Kraftwerk came together) was in West Germany, which had closer links to modern Europe. You can hear French alongside German lyrics in 'Trans-Europe Express', a sign of the growing relationships across Europe. The song talks about travelling through Europe, meeting in Paris (France) and stopping off in Vienna (Austria) before returning to Germany.

It's no surprise that Kraftwerk's electronic sounds captured the imaginations of music makers for years to come. Right up until the present day, you'll hear the echoes of Kraftwerk in popular music that uses electronic sounds rather than traditional instruments. If you drew a map of modern music and all its branches, you'd have to put Kraftwerk somewhere in the middle.

Why is Kraftwerk important? Dreaming of the future is how humans change the world, coming up with new ideas and visons for how things could be. At a time when the political world was still healing, Kraftwerk's music was like a symbol of modern Europe.

It's a wonderfully optimistic thing: to think about what the world could be like and actually try to make it happen. Without these ideas, humanity can never move forward. Also, I think it's important that Kraftwerk has influenced so many different genres of music, including hip-hop, punk, techno, dance, pop, rock and funk, from different artists in different places, across multiple generations. Proof, again, that despite all the divisions, we really are living in one musical world.

'I Feel Love'

Donna Summer (1977)

Question: What's so scary about entering a new musical world?

Music, even a single song, can be an invitation into a whole world that you might not feel like you belong to. Think about it. Think about how a song can allow you, for a few short minutes, to live a life you have never led. Just by humming along or reciting the lyrics, you can join a community that might be hundreds of miles away, or years in the past.

In this way, making a song in a particular genre (or style) of music can be like making a portal into a whole world.

In the 1970s, the world of disco was alive and well. Disco was an exciting type of dance music that had become popular in New York City. It was fast and electric, with pounding drums and instruments that sound like glowing neon lights in the rain. It's also fun and upbeat, with a simple repeated drum rhythm that is very easy to dance to. As a result, disco was perfect modern dance music – inviting everyone to get on the dance floor and follow an irresistible groove.

Like all musical styles, disco has deep cultural roots, stretching back into Africa and Latin America. Perhaps for this reason, disco was first popular among groups of people who were seen as on the edge of society, or *marginalised*. This included the black and Latin communities of New York, but it was also popular among gay communities who were treated with discrimination and prejudice by the non-gay, or 'straight', mainstream. This meant that early disco was often heard in nightclubs where gay people met to have a good time.

It was a whole new world: a world where it was OK to be gay, where you could relax into your sexuality without the fear of being judged. What 'The Twist' had started in the early 1960s had now developed into a whole subculture of music and dance. The old rules of dancing in strict boy/girl couples were ancient history, and this came with a pulsing, funky disco soundtrack.

Many famous disco songs feature vocals from black American women. One theory behind this is that black female vocalists often sing in an expressive style that feels as free as disco audiences wanted to feel. It's a lovely idea: that music can be the soundtrack to your soul, allowing you to pour your feelings into the sounds you hear. In the 1970s, Donna Summer was already an established recording artist. It wasn't until she met an Italian-born man called Giorgio Moroder and an English-born man called Pete Bellotte that she would become a disco legend. The year was 1977, and the three met by chance in Germany, the country where Kraftwerk had pioneered a whole new electronic sound.

'I Feel Love' is a fusion of classic disco, Donna's soaring vocals and electronic music production. Put together, it sounded like nothing anyone had heard before. It sounds like robots and holograms and flying cars in the future, while ancient drums beat in the background, like a religious ritual. You can barely make out Donna's words as she wails and warbles, but you can absolutely feel the power of . . . *love?*

Just listening to this song takes you into the world of 1970s New York. It feels like entry into a nocturnal world that would have scared so many people – a world where it was OK to be gay and you didn't have to follow society's rules. In an important way, 'I Feel Love' was like an invitation into a marginalised culture, which might explain the song's huge success. Not only did it introduce a whole new era of electronic dance music (EDM), but it also brought disco to the front of the picture.

By the end of the 1970s, disco had become one of the most popular genres of music in the USA and many other parts of the world too. Disco records were being produced and sold in massive numbers, changing the landscape of modern, popular music. But a lot of people still didn't trust it. Its associations with black communities, Latin communities and gay culture in particular led to homophobia and racism – plain and simple. In 1979, the true extent of these feelings was revealed in a notorious event that has come to be known as Disco Demolition Night, which took place at a baseball stadium in Chicago. In between two games, two things happened:

- A huge box was filled with disco records, and . . .
- . . . the records were destroyed – in an explosion.

There are still arguments over why Disco Demolition Night happened. Some people believe that it was a reaction to the fact that disco was becoming too popular. Others say that it was an act of discrimination from people who didn't want society to change. Destroying disco records could be symbolic of a fear and hatred for everything that disco represented. Ultimately, this was a violent event, drawing negative energy from the crowd and inviting them to turn into a mob. In 1977, Donna Summer sang about feeling love, and two years later, you had disco music being destroyed with hate. And hatred never built anything positive.

Listen again to 'I Feel Love'. But this time, imagine you are someone who is scared of the future, scared of change. What does it sound like now? Disorientating? Aggressive? Uncertain? Strange? It's likely that at least one copy of 'I Feel Love' was included in the Disco Demolition Night, just when popular music was ready to evolve into something new.

'Aux armes et caetera'

Serge Gainsbourg (1979)

Question: Can a song challenge history?

In 1979, Serge Gainsbourg was already a very successful musician in his home country of France, but he wasn't quite yet a *superstar*.

His most famous song so far was a duet called 'Je t'aime ... moi non plus' ('I love you ... me neither') with a singer and actress called Jane Birkin, who was his girlfriend at the time. Serge had also become well known by making songs that were sometimes recorded by other artists. His music was always very emotional, often full of yearning, and sometimes playful, but he had yet to find that one big hit to make him a massive household name all over the world.

In his quest to create something new that would take his musical career further, Serge looked towards the Caribbean for an answer.

We'll look carefully at reggae in the next chapter. It's a genre of music that originates from Jamaica, which is where Serge travelled to on his new musical mission. In Kingston, the capital city, he struck up a relationship with some of the best reggae musicians of the day. Together, they came up with songs that were pure reggae through and through, with Lowell Dunbar's shuffling drums, Robbie Shakespeare's pulsing bass guitar, and electric organ stabs by Ansel Collins. The recipe was a winner. But Serge had something extra special to add to the mix . . .

For one of the new songs, Serge decided to draw inspiration from his own country's national anthem, 'La Marseillaise'. It's a piece of music that goes back to 1792, with lyrics written by an army officer called Claude Joseph Rouget de Lisle, just after France declared war against Austria. As far as national anthems go, 'La

Marseillaise' is very energetic indeed, full of soaring melodies and a marching rhythm that makes you feel like you're striding into battle. Its lyrics are violent too, with references to ferocious soldiers, blood and taking up weapons against an enemy who is 'impure'.

Really and truly, the tone and content of 'La Marseillaise' is far, far away from the laid-back groove of reggae music. But Serge decided to put them together. In fact, he took the most dramatic part of the national anthem, where you sing 'Aux armes! Citoyens' (which means 'Citizens! To arms!') and made that the main hook of his new reggae song.

The song was a hit. It was one of the first popular reggae songs to be heard widely across Europe and got everyone talking about Serge Gainsbourg – the unlikely reggae star.

But not everyone was happy.

Some people thought that the song was insulting towards France. They thought that Serge was being disrespectful towards 'La Marseillaise' and making fun of its message. For these people, the 'et caetera' part of the song's title felt like Serge was deliberately poking fun at the national anthem's lyrics by failing to spell them out fully. These were serious accusations. It got so serious that Serge actually received death threats.

Here, we can just see how powerful a sense of national identity can be. By making a playful version of the French national anthem, Serge Gainsbourg created a dangerous situation for himself, even though the song itself, recorded by real reggae artists, was pure and honest.

Two years after recording 'Aux armes et caetera', Serge found a way to answer his critics. He found an original copy of the manuscript for 'La Marseillaise', in an auction, and he bought it. Then he showed the world what this original manuscript said. It said . . .

'. . . aux armes et caetera.'

The original composer hadn't wanted to keep writing the whole 'aux armes, citoyens' over and over again, so he just wrote 'et caetera' to save time. In a funny sort of way, Serge's disrespectful lyrics were more accurate than people had thought!

This story is a wonderful example of how broad the musical world can be. A French artist, working with Jamaican musicians to help bring reggae into Europe through lyrics to a national anthem that was composed 187 years before. 'Aux armes et caetera' is a song that you can enjoy as a slice of reggae, or as a kind of criticism against the violence of military power. It makes you dance, but it makes you think, with Serge's gravelly spoken vocals alongside the beautiful voices of Marcia Griffiths, Rita Marley and Judy Mowatt. It's light but deep. It's fun but serious. And for Serge Gainsbourg, it was a moment of true musical freedom.

'Redemption Song'

Bob Marley (1980)

Question: When will we be truly free?

When you think about where reggae started, it's amazing how far it's come.

Reggae began in the Caribbean island of Jamaica in the 1960s, which might be before you were born but wasn't actually all that long ago. Reggae was a new type of music that borrowed from traditional styles such as ska and mento but was altogether unique. It's dance music, but it's laid-back and relaxing, with a rolling groove, jangly guitars, deep bass and a funky, offbeat rhythm.

Reggae sounds like sunshine, beaches, nightclubs and partying, which is part of the reason that it became so popular. But it also sounds like protest and change. One of the key features of reggae has always been looking at society and asking deep questions about the way things are. At its heart, reggae is *socially conscious* music, meaning that it is aware that there are problems in the world. It's not simply about having a good time.

By the end of the 1970s, reggae had become internationally known. One of the biggest reasons for this was a film called *The Harder They Come*, with a soundtrack by its star actor, Jimmy Cliff. The film showed people everywhere about some of the hardships faced by young Jamaican people, while also introducing hit reggae songs to new audiences.

Undoubtedly, the biggest star in reggae just happens to be one of the biggest stars in popular music history. His name is Robert Nesta Marley, born in 1945, and he wrote songs and performed under the name 'Bob'. A legend.

You've heard Bob Marley. You've heard his music in the way that you've heard national anthems and nursery rhymes. With his band, the Wailers, Bob Marley made the kind of music that travelled like a breeze. One of the first big hits by Bob Marley and the Wailers was a song from 1965 called 'One Love'. It's a beautiful song that asks us to be one people together and feel all right. Remember, Bob grew up in a world that was only starting to recover from the Second World War, in a country that was still part of the British Empire. The optimism of sharing one global love is a message that was, and is, truly inspirational.

When you look at a picture of Bob Marley you'll notice that his hair is in long, thick locks, which is the hairstyle worn by *Rastafarian* men. It was during the 1960s that Bob Marley began to believe in the teachings of *Rastafari*. If you haven't heard of it, Rastafari is a spiritual belief system that goes back to Jamaica in the 1930s. Rastafarians believe in a single god, called *Jah*. They also believe the Western world, including Europe, to be *Babylon*, which is a reference from the Christian Bible to a place of suffering. The idea is simple: that black people in the modern world experience suffering in a white world. In this sense, Rastafari is Afrocentric, focusing on Africa (or *Zion*) as the 'promised land', or the true human home.

Emancipation: The process of being set free.

In 1979, some of these ideas were put forward in a Bob Marley song called 'Zimbabwe'. It speaks of how everyone has the right to decide their own destiny and calls for liberation of Africa. When you think about how Africa has been treated by Babylon since the scramble for Africa, into slavery and beyond, you realise that these are very big ideas indeed.

In 1980, one year before Bob Marley died, 'Redemption Song' was given to the world. It was the last track on the twelfth and final album by Bob Marley and the Wailers, entitled *Uprising*, which takes us right back to the ideas of protest and liberation.

Prophet: A wise and inspirational person who explains visions of the future.

Unlike other songs, 'Redemption Song' features only Bob Marley's voice and a solitary guitar. It's a song that invites you to listen – really listen – to his words of pain, hope and beauty. Marley takes us on a journey that starts with the desperation of being forced into slavery, which we know actually happened to millions of black people. Then he asks us to free ourselves from mental slavery and trust in Jah, the almighty, before reminding us that only we can free our own minds, by singing songs of freedom. He talks about the death of prophets who can help guide our paths, killed by people trying to control us. And, again, he asks for help to sing these songs.

111

When Bob Marley wrote 'Redemption Song', he knew he was dying from cancer. This is a fact that makes the song even more poignant and powerful. One version of the story goes that Bob just turned up at the studio one day with a new song to share, and played it once through for the engineer. Then he played and sang it again, this time recorded. Which is the version we can listen to now.

Redemption: The act of saving, or being saved, from sin, evil, or wrongdoing.

There's something urgent but somehow peaceful about this song that makes it feel like an anthem of hope. To be free is the greatest privilege a person can have. Think about it. The freedom to live and love and grow – it's all we ever need. The world can choke our freedoms in so many ways, but, like Bob says, we can free ourselves from these ways of thinking. And a song like this can light the way. You don't have to be Jamaican, or Rastafari, or black to listen to 'Redemption Song' and feel this energy. Listening to it now as I type these words, it feels as powerful to me now as I'm sure it did to anyone else who has heard it and anyone else who ever will.

So let this one play out long and loud. Because sometimes, our songs are all we'll ever have.

'Under Pressure'

Queen and David Bowie (1981)

Question: How can a song help us to break free?

In 1992, on Monday 20 April, 72,000 people gathered at Wembley Stadium in London, England, for one of the biggest concerts of the year. It was a tribute concert, for a singer called Freddie Mercury, who had died a year earlier in 1991.

Freddie Mercury died of AIDS. AIDS is an acronym for something called the acquired immune deficiency syndrome, which is linked to the human immunodeficiency virus (HIV). People with HIV might not show any signs of being ill at first, but the later stages of infection can include serious health complications that can ultimately lead to death.

The earliest signs of AIDS and the HIV infection were first recognised by scientists in the USA back in 1981. It is believed that the infection originated from primates in some parts of west and central Africa, before making the jump to humans. As of 2020, it is thought that somewhere near 37 million people across the world are living with HIV. Thankfully, medical progress since the 1980s means that it is possible to live a long and healthy life with the virus.

It wasn't always this way. In the 1980s, an HIV and AIDS pandemic caused a panic across many parts of the world. Even worse, many people started targeting specific groups of people and accusing them of spreading AIDS, effectively blaming them for the disease. One of these groups was gay people, who were fiercely discriminated against even though anyone can transmit HIV (through sexual intercourse, blood or even between mother and child during pregnancy). When I was growing up in the 1980s, there was so much ignorance surrounding HIV and AIDS. Lots of people thought you could catch it by kissing or even touching skin, while many believed that it was some kind of 'gay disease'. They were totally wrong.

Discrimination against gay people is part of a deeper social problem called *homophobia*, which literally means the fear of homosexual (or 'gay') people. It's a senseless type of prejudice that still affects societies all over the world to this day. It was so bad that many gay celebrities used to pretend not to be gay, for fear of losing their support. Elton John, who we met a few chapters ago, revealed to the world that he was gay in 1992, at the age of forty-five.

Even worse, when gay men contracted AIDS, they were often treated as though they had done something wrong and left to die in appalling conditions. This is both immoral and cruel.

Freddie Mercury was diagnosed with AIDS in 1987, but he only announced his diagnosis in 1991, the day before he died.

We shouldn't think of Freddie Mercury as simply someone who died from AIDS. He was an electrifying singer and performer, part of a rock group called Queen who had a string of hits throughout the 1970s and 1980s. His voice was like lightning doing acrobatics, and his performances were full of power. This, more than anything, is why thousands of people gathered to honour his memory, while also raising awareness of AIDS. The concert was a celebration of life through song, with a whole selection of music superstars coming out to perform with Freddie's band.

'Under Pressure' starts with the word *Pressure!* almost screamed in frustration, before a reminder that pressure is pushing down on me and you both, which is very true. The way the world is, we're all under all kinds of pressures that we didn't create: the pressure to succeed, the pressure to act a certain way, the pressure to survive, the pressure to fit in.

There are so many powerful moments in this song. One is when Freddie Mercury and David Bowie say *let me out*, together. It sounds like a cry for help. For gay people, right up to this day, there's an idea that you have to 'come out', which means revealing your sexuality to the world. In a way, this is an unfair burden to put on people. It suggests that you can't just be accepted for who you are without getting the OK from people around you. And we all want to be accepted. The lyrics then talk about the terror of knowing what this world is all about, making you think about all the pain and hatred that we can't seem to get away from. Later on in the song, Freddie asks why we can't give love another chance, repeating the question into an endless echo . . .

It's as true now as it was in 1981, when homophobia was preventing gay people from living free and happy lives, when sexism meant that women and girls were still struggling to be treated with equal respect, when the UK was gripped by protests and riots linked to racial discrimination and social unrest. In 1981, people really were out on the streets screaming for a better world. Why can't we give love? A love which, in the words of David Bowie, *dares us to care?*

The Freddie Mercury tribute concert proved that people did care. Watching the footage now, I'm struck by how much of an emotional release it was, with the crowd of thousands pouring energy back towards the stage. It's at moments like this that you realise how meaningful change is fully possible, if only enough people join together in their beliefs.

Today, we still have homophobia, and the fight for LGBTQ+ rights continues. But there is far more tolerance and understanding, with new pressures to do better. The problems of the world won't just disappear by magic. If we continue to put the world under pressure to improve, then maybe it will.

'The Message'

Grandmaster Flash and the Furious Five (1982)

Question: Is it possible to make something out of nothing?

Picture it:

Broken glass is everywhere . . . It's noisy and dirty all the time . . . Bad smells . . . Dangerous people lurking around corners, waiting to attack you . . . Rats and cockroaches . . . People are even going to the toilet in the streets . . . and you with no choice but to stay there anyway.

This is the scene that is set in Melle Mel's opening verse to the song 'The Message'.

When you think about rap music, you might think of big cars, gold chains, money and a flashy lifestyle. Nowadays, that is what a lot of popular rap music seems to be all about. But it didn't start this way. In fact, the origins of hip-hop started with the exact opposite, hence the opening lines to this song.

The 1970s was not the most optimistic time for poor communities living in big American cities. Years of poverty meant that black African American and Hispanic people (of South American heritage) were living through tough times. Urban environments were often overcrowded, with a lack of facilities. This also came with other social problems such as unemployment and crime, affecting people of all ages. Some people have called this an 'urban jungle' – the same jungle that is described at the start of this song.

It was in this seemingly depressing environment that something called hip-hop would be born. And hip-hop is far from depressing. It actually started with a party.

A history of hip-hop

New York is full of streets arranged into a strict pattern of grids. Much of the housing is in tower blocks, where communities live very closely together. In the heat of those simmering East Coast summers, block parties would invite whole neighbourhoods to party in the streets. Just like anywhere in the world where people don't have much money, we'll still find ways to celebrate life and join together.

The music at these parties would be provided by disc jockeys or 'DJs', who got that name because they played, or 'jockeyed', vinyl discs. One locally famous DJ was Clive Campbell, who went by the name of DJ Kool Herc. Kool Herc was originally from Jamaica, where there was a tradition of MCs talking or 'toasting' over music to keep the crowd moving. He brought this tradition with him to parties in New York, but he also brought something new, a musical innovation that would change everything, forever.

Rather than playing one record on one turntable, Kool Herc used two turntables at the same time. Why? Because it allowed him to play the funkiest part of the same song back to back, using fast fingers to drop the needle at the start of the 'break' (when only drums are playing). Looping the breaks was the start of hip-hop culture. Suddenly, you could dance to the funkiest part of a song, forever! These raw, extended drum breaks gave the perfect opportunity for MCs to talk in rhyme for minutes at a time, *rapping* into the microphone. In Jamaica, *deejaying* was the name given to speaking over the music (not to be confused with DJing records). Meanwhile, dancers were inventing wild new moves to dance to the drum breaks, which came to be known as *breakdancing*.

There were other types of expression too. Young artists began using colourful cans of spray paint to create huge pieces of art known as graffiti, on walls and even subway trains. It was illegal activity, so graffiti artists took it as a badge of honour to have their art up in the city for all to see. And then came a whole new fashion, based on the sportswear that young people liked to wear.

Hip-hop had arrived. It was given that name because of the 'hippity-hop' style of talking that rappers would use on the mic. This was a moment of innovation in the face of oppression, where marginalised groups invented something new and exciting out of the limited resources available. Hip-hop would go on to become the most successful black American cultural export since rock 'n' roll, spreading across the whole world and influencing modern music forever.

In early hip-hop, the DJ was the most important person, because the DJ was the one who was controlling the music. This is why Grandmaster Flash is listed first: because he was the DJ, responsible for the backbone of the song. Early hip-hop DJs would obsess about their records, using samples from older songs to create something new. In this way, hip-hop is an example of music being in conversation with itself, throughout history. Produced in 1982, 'The Message' actually doesn't contain many samples. However, another hip-hop classic from 1982 is 'Planet Rock' by Afrika Bambaataa, which contains lots of samples, including Kraftwerk's 'Trans-Europe Express' that we heard back on page [94]. In a way that we have never seen before, hip-hop reaches into the musical world and comes out with all kinds of unexpected combinations.

This is what the makes 'The Message' all the more important. It goes beyond the party, the celebration and the creativity, using hip-hop to say very important things. It talks about deep social problems and the difficulties of living a second-rate life. It puts you in the position of young black Americans being harassed by the police. It warns against the risks of dropping out of school and ends with the chilling image of a death in a prison cell. It reminds us that life has an edge that you don't want to get close to, all while pulsing to a rhythm you can dance to.

Hip-hop's combination of joy and struggle is what makes it continue to be relevant into the twenty-first century. At more than forty years old, hip-hop still feels fresh, new and exciting, because being inventive is part of its DNA. But it also has the power to reflect upon social problems and invite us to think about suffering in the modern world, from people who are sidelined and underprivileged.

Hip-hop changed the world. Keep an ear open for it in the music we'll continue to meet along the way.

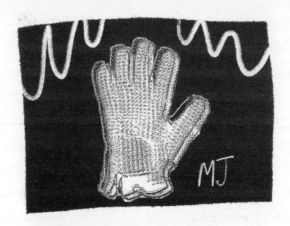

'Billie Jean'

Michael Jackson (1982)

Question: How did black culture make it into the pop mainstream?

When Michael Jackson released the album *Thriller* in November 1982, there's no way he could have known that it was going to be one of the biggest albums, in any genre, of all time. There's no way he could have predicted that it would break records for sales all over the world, or that it would set the standard for what a pop record could be.

And yet, that's exactly what happened. And all these years later, *Thriller* is still one of the most successful musical releases in pop music history.

Michael Jackson was always ambitious. As a child, he was the star of a family group called the Jackson 5, along with his brothers Jackie, Tito, Jermaine and Marlon. This means that he was used to not only making music but being a performing artist from a very young age, led by his determined father, Joe. Soon, young Michael was ready to take on the world as a solo artist, which he did with his first album since leaving the Jackson 5, *Off the Wall*, from 1979.

It was an instant classic, full of hit songs with smooth, soulful vocals from Michael himself. The album was produced by the highly celebrated songwriter and musician Quincy Jones, a true legend in black American music. And this is the thing: from the outset, Michael Jackson made *black* music. *Thriller* took pieces of rock, disco and R & B to create something exciting and new – a sound unlike anything the world had heard before. Michael's biggest influences included soul singers such as James Brown, a funk and soul pioneer who would dazzle audiences with his electrifying dance moves and sweat-dripping performances. Inspired by James Brown, Michael quickly established himself as one of the best performers the world has ever seen, grabbing audiences with his intense routines.

This is a huge part of the reason for his incredible success. No one in the world of music could perform with his style and intensity, which he had developed over his whole life. By the time *Thriller* was recorded, Michael Jackson was ready to take his throne as the so-called 'King of Pop'.

But was the world ready to let him?

As a creator of black music, Michael Jackson had barriers and limits placed on his success. This is how racism works – it prevents people who are racially marginalised from reaching their full potential. There is a reason that before Michael Jackson, black artists in America had struggled to see the kind of world-beating success that he would create. For people worldwide, Michael Jackson would become a symbol of black success.

A turning point in this journey came about in a music show on television called *Motown 25*. It was here that Michael Jackson performed 'Billie Jean', live, and it blew people away. Wearing a black sequinned jacket and his trademark shiny glove, Michael sang his song and, more importantly, did *the moonwalk*.

Whoa.

If you're anywhere near my age, you'll know why I'm pausing for effect. The moonwalk was an impossibly smooth dance move that looked like Michael Jackson was sliding backwards while walking forward. It was originally taken from breakdancing, something that Michael Jackson would have been inspired by as a dancer, but when he did it on that stage, it became his trademark move. Suddenly, children all over the world wanted to be like Michael Jackson by moonwalking like he did. A star was born.

Just by existing as a black, pop music superstar, Michael Jackson was political whether he liked it or not. In the 1980s, the biggest music channel on television was MTV (Music Television). MTV did not play black artists. The bosses at MTV felt as though black music was not mainstream enough for their (mainly white) audience. As a result, black American artists didn't have the MTV platform to showcase their music, meaning that they would have to 'cross over', or find some way of appealing to white audiences.

With *Thriller*, Michael Jackson proved beyond all doubt that he had endless crossover appeal, and on 10 March 1983, the video to 'Billie Jean' was shown on MTV. Later that year, the full video to the song 'Thriller' was also shown, confirming what everyone already knew – that Michael Jackson was a true superstar. As a video, 'Thriller' is ambitious and creative. It runs thirteen minutes long and is basically a whole movie, complete with special effects and scary scenes. It's a fantastic piece of horror, where Michael is out on a date and, oops, turns into a zombie. A dancing zombie. With a whole team of other dancing zombies behind him.

Yes, *Thriller* is a lot of fun, but Michael's life was not free of worry. It contained a lot of pain: his lonely childhood, his reclusive life as a megastar and accusations about serious wrongdoings in his private life. He is also famous for becoming lighter in complexion over the years, a process he went through because of a skin condition called vitiligo. But ultimately, as he asked in a hit song from 1991, does it really matter if you're 'black' or 'white' anyway?

Since 'Billie Jean', black music has had permanent crossover appeal. Michael Jackson proved that pop music rooted in black American styles could be successful not only in America but all over the world. He created a standard for pop that artists are still trying to reach today, with a template that has been copied over and over and over again. If you look closely at many of the biggest pop artists of the day, you will see echoes of Michael's moves in their performances and ideas.

Powerful vocals, smooth dance moves, big ensemble dance choreography and wildly creative flair. And he did all this as an artist who had to tackle racism within the industry that he grew up in. In this sense, the success of *Thriller* was a moment of justice for black culture in the white mainstream, where blackness was, finally, given permission to shine.

'Do They Know It's Christmas'

Band Aid (1984)

Question: What does charity sound like?

Aid = what you give to people who need help.

A band = a group of people who make music.

A Band-Aid = what people from the USA call a plaster.

A plaster = something you put over a wound to help it to heal.

Band Aid = a group of musicians making music to try to help.

In 1983, Ethiopia (in east Africa) was hit by famine. It was the worst famine in over a century and lasted for a full two years. The famine was devastating, killing hundreds of thousands of people and leaving many more without homes or basic utilities. Part of the reason for this disaster was drought, whereby a lack of water made it impossible to grow crops for food. Another reason is civil war, whereby fighting within Ethiopia had been making the country unstable for years.

I remember seeing images of the Ethiopian famine on television. The news would show horrific images of death and starvation, with skeletal children too weak to even move. It was difficult to watch and showed people in the UK how bad things were for so many ordinary Ethiopian people.

One person who was moved by these images of suffering was a singer called Bob Geldof. He and his wife, Paula Yates, decided to try to help, through music. The plan was simple: to assemble a group of musicians to record a special song for charity, with all proceeds going to help the victims of famine in Ethiopia. The song that was recorded was called 'Do They Know It's Christmas', and the supergroup that Bob assembled was called Band Aid.

'Do They Know It's Christmas' was recorded in

twenty-four hours, with a line-up of the biggest stars in music at the time. The song was a massive hit, selling millions of copies worldwide and leading to a huge live charity concert in 1985 called Live Aid. Combined, Band Aid and Live Aid raised tens of millions of pounds for the famine relief effort.

When I was growing up, images of Africa on the TV always showed it to be a place of suffering, with starving children, no technology and mud huts. In reality, African countries are a combination of great technology, progress, innovation, wealth and rich cultural history, alongside social problems such as poverty, which exist everywhere. By presenting Africa as a 'third world' full of 'developing' nations, the idea is upheld that Africa is less important than the West. The lyrics to 'Do They Know It's Christmas' are naive and ignorant in this way. They talk about how, in Africa, nothing ever grows, and there is no water, which might describe drought and famine, but is nothing like the reality of the whole African continent.

Band Aid was a huge moment for global humanitarianism, and clearly a kind act of charity from the UK, towards Africa. But it raises questions about the huge power imbalances that have been created in our world. African as a continent is not seen as equal to

Europe. From a European perspective, African countries are often seen as helpless and broken, in constant need of charity, a situation that goes as far back as the seventeenth century, when racist ideas began to split the world up into categories based on ethnicity and skin colour. For centuries, Africa has been seen as beneath Europe, and this is by design. Seeing Africa in this way allowed European countries to justify treating African people as subhuman, up to and including using them as slaves. The echoes of this way of thinking can still be seen in the idea that Africa, as a whole, is a place that cannot help itself, even though the situation is nowhere near as simple as this.

Over the years, 'Do They Know It's Christmas' has become less popular as people have realised its complex relationship with Africa. This doesn't mean that trying to help people in need is ever a bad idea. The Band Aid project remains a significant moment, where musicians did the job of world leaders, and this might be something to be proud of.

The way that Africa is seen by the West remains tied up in broken stereotypes and outdated ideas. It's all linked to the fact that Africa, as a continent, has been the victim of exploitation throughout history, with a lot of African nations struggling to establish themselves as a result. Remember, many African countries that were created in the nineteenth century were made by European colonisers who had no respect for the kingdoms and communities who were already living there. Hopefully, as time goes on, the relationship between seemingly powerful countries and their less powerful counterparts is becoming better understood, with pity and ignorance being replaced by understanding and respect. And given time, we might find deeper solutions to the complex problems that power and greed have created in our world.

'Under Mi Sleng Teng'

Wayne Smith (1985)

Question: What do you get if you mix technology, cultures and different styles of music?

Once upon a time, in a country called Jamaica, there was a young man called Noel Davey who liked making music.

To make his music, Noel wanted to buy a new piece of equipment: a digital synthesizer called the Yamaha DX7. Unfortunately, the Yamaha DX7 was too expensive for Noel to afford, so he had to settle on a cheaper solution: an electronic keyboard called the Casio MT-40.

One of Noel's friends was a teenager called Wayne Smith. Wayne loved to sing reggae songs, and the two friends enjoyed working together. One day, they came up with a brand-new song, which used a preset on Noel's Casio keyboard. A preset is a melody that is built into an electronic keyboard. All you have to do is press a button and the keyboard plays a little electronic tune that goes on loop forever.

Noel and Wayne's song was based on the 'Rock' preset. It was an addictive rhythm, made up of the computerised sounds of the Casio MT-40. They took the song to a music producer called King Jammy (whose real name was Lloyd James). King Jammy liked what he heard but thought he could improve it by slowing it down a notch and adding some drums and piano. When he'd finished, they called the song 'Under Mi Sleng Teng' (which is a reference to being under the influence of cannabis).

The song was good. In fact, the song was so good that it became a hit record. The tune and melody became known as the 'Sleng Teng' *riddim*, which is a patois expression meaning 'rhythm'. A riddim is a tune that can be used by anyone to make a new song of their own. Sleng Teng was so popular that in time, hundreds of artists would us it. A whole new way of making reggae music had been born, using electronic sounds and cheap technology.

Once upon another time, years before 'Under Mi Sleng Teng', a young woman called Hiroko Okuda went to a music college in Tokyo, Japan, to start studying musicology. As you might imagine, Hiroko was a big fan of music, so much so that she wanted to study it in detail.

Eventually, Hiroko completed her course and got a job at an electronics company called Casio. Her first project upon joining Casio was in the development of a new keyboard: the model MT-40. Hiroko programmed a preset rhythm on the Casio MT-40, which was called the 'Rock' preset.

Hiroko's 'Rock' preset was inspired by a song, but it's not entirely clear which one. One version of the story says that it was a song called 'Somethin' Else' by Eddie Cochran (from 1959). Another version says that it was 'Hang On to Yourself' by David Bowie (from 1971). A third version says it might have been 'Anarchy in the UK' by the Sex Pistols (from 1976). Either way, the twist to this story is more incredible than any of these suggestions. It turns out that before young Hiroko Okuda went to work at Casio she was a fan of reggae. Yep, the same genre of music that Noel Davey would reinvent with his cheap keyboard, years later. The fact that the 'Rock' preset sounds a bit like reggae in the first place might not be a coincidence. She liked reggae. She liked it so much that she even wrote a big essay about it while studying at university. Let that sink in for a moment.

Jamaica and Japan might start with the same letter, but they are very different places. They are in different parts of the world and come with histories of two very different cultures. Yet, through the Sleng Teng riddim, a love of reggae and the digital technology of a Casio keyboard, these two countries are united forever.

I love the story behind 'Under Mi Sleng Teng'. I love how it weaves such different experiences together through the power of music. I love how it's hard to work out what came first, and what inspired who to create music that changed the world. I love how it proves, once again, that creativity and connections are often the best of what humans can offer. This chapter is proof that we live in a whole world of music.

'Homeless'

Paul Simon with Ladysmith Black Mambazo (1986)

Question: What makes Africa a home for humanity?

What are we learning so far?

We're learning that music is indeed a global language. We're learning that musical styles can travel across borders and through time. We're learning that the world can be a deeply unfair place, full of inequality that comes from different groups seeking power and control.

We're also learning that the twentieth century was a time when the West was firmly established as dominant, with whiteness positioned as superior to blackness.

These racial ideas can be seen clearly in South Africa, a country that has, in the past, been torn apart by racist ideas. We've already discussed the concept of apartheid, which saw the legal separation of South African people according to the colour of their skin. In the 1980s, apartheid was very much alive in South Africa. It was drawing continued criticism from other countries who were making a stand against what was thought to be unfair. One way of doing this was to boycott South Africa, which meant refusing to support South African trade. The boycott was set in place by the United Nations, and began in 1962.

So when someone called Paul Simon decided to record an album in South Africa, which meant breaking the boycott completely, it was a hugely political moment. Paul Simon was a very successful, white, American musician. He had already recorded six albums, with a string of hit songs in his catalogue. However, his sixth album hadn't done as well as the ones before, and he was looking for new inspiration.

In 1985, Paul Simon flew to the city of Johannesburg in South Africa after being inspired by South African street music that he had heard on a cassette tape back in the USA. It was there that he set about recording his new album, called *Graceland*, which was a made with local South African musicians.

In Johannesburg, he had to learn a whole new musical language, experimenting with rhythms, sounds and words that were foreign to him, as a white Westerner. One example is *mbaqanga*, a jazzy style of South African music with roots in Zulu traditions. Here, Paul Simon found himself making something that was totally new to him, using styles that had existed in Africa for generations. He was also welcomed by South African music groups including Ladysmith Black Mambazo, who sang on *Graceland* and would later go on tour with Paul Simon, performing live. This, again, highlights the power of music to build bridges between different people. And to be honest, it also highlights the power of money and fame – Paul Simon was easily able to use his status and reputation as a passport into a new musical world.

But let's get into the tricky stuff:

Was Paul Simon borrowing African styles because he'd run out of ideas?

Was he doing what many white musicians had done already for decades – imitating black music for white audiences?

Or was he doing something positive in creating a platform for black, African artists living in a country gripped by anti-black racism?

It's complicated. On the one hand *Graceland* is clearly a celebration of traditional black South African culture, which had been marginalised by apartheid. On the other more cynical hand, you could say that it represents a white, Western artist exploiting African culture for his own benefit. On the *other* other hand (we have three hands now), *Graceland* can be seen as a meeting point between Western and African traditions, blended through music. These aren't easy knots to unpick and I can see how all three perspectives make sense.

But when I go think back to my childhood, seeing footage of 'Homeless' being performed on a crackly VHS video cassette, I remember being amazed at hearing *African* sounds in mainstream music. I remember hearing Ladysmith Black Mambazo for the first time, with a chorus of voices that seemed to vibrate through my whole body. As someone of African heritage myself, I felt proud, and moved, even as a little kid. 'Homeless' is haunting and hopeful, with poetic lyrics about life and death that make you think hard about the struggles being faced by South African people. And at the end, all you can do is cry out why, why, why? There is beauty and pain in this song that makes it so much bigger than the arguments over Paul Simon's intentions.

For millions of people all over the world, including Paul Simon, *Graceland* was a moment of discovery, a musical moment of South Africa being seen as whole. With its simplicity of voices, with no instruments in the background, 'Homeless' feels like a very honest and open part of this conversation. And really, it's a reminder that songs can bring us to a place of calm, even if they are made at a time of confusion.

'Pacific State'

808 State (1989)

Question: Can the world move to a single beat?

One, two, three, four.
One, two, three, four.
One, two, three, four.
One, two, three, four.

It's that simple. And sometimes, the most simple things have the most impact. Like counting one, two, three, four, over and over again.

This is a book about music throughout time, but I realise we haven't spent a lot of time on music theory, how music works, how songs are built, that kind of thing. So let's go there for a moment.

Counting to four is the basis of the vast majority of music in Western culture. These counts, or beats, are the backbone for music across genres. When you get four beats together, it's called a bar. If you like rap music, like me, you might have heard rappers talking about *spitting bars*, which just means rapping to a set rhythm of bars over time.

In 'Pacific State', you can hear four beats in a bar, with a kick drum hitting on each beat, over and over again. The kick drum is the biggest part of a drumkit, operated with a pedal that whacks a mallet against a huge drum that sits on the floor. It's a big, booming sound, like the thud of an excited heartbeat.

When you get four of these beats in a regular, even sequence, it's known as 'four to the floor' – probably because the drum keeps returning like a stamping foot. Keep this up for a while and you have the basis of a whole genre of music. Welcome to *dance music*.

There is something universal about a four to the floor rhythm. You can clap it out easily. It's flat and even. It's constant too, never changing. So it's easy to follow. This is a big part of the reason that four to the floor has been such a popular rhythm when it comes to dancing. We see it in disco from the 1970s, which was all about fun and freedom on the dance floor, inviting people to dance, together to one groove.

The word 'together' is important here too. Remember, before popular music pulsed to a drumbeat, dancing (in Europe) was a formal, quite serious situation, to be done between a male and female partner, following specific rules. As we saw with Chubby Checker's twist, new music loosened the rules and suddenly, people could dance side by side, with anyone they wanted. The development of four to the floor opened this up even more, inviting whole dance floors to move to the rhythm in free-flowing unison, guided by a strong and steady four-beat drum.

Pacific State is part of a legacy of something called *house music*: electronic music that transformed modern dance music forever. House was invented by black DJs and producers in the 1980s, and it was named after the Warehouse, a club in Chicago where the music was first played.

Technology has always been a massive part of the musical story. Without the invention of new instruments, new musical ideas might never be born. Going as far back to the invention of the pianoforte, known as the piano (which allowed composers to create a whole range of sounds on one instrument), the tools to make music have always been as important as the different styles of music themselves. To this very day, a piano keyboard is still one of the most common ways of creating new electronic music and controlling digital sounds – you've probably used one at school.

Technology was one reason that house music spread so quickly. The '808' part of the name 'Pacific 808' refers to an electronic drum machine called the TR-808, made by a company called Roland. This machine offered musicians a way of making electronic dance music easily and affordably, with heavy drums and a playground of electronic sounds to explore.

The beauty of this song is that it sounds like much more than a bunch of computerised sounds, even though it is entirely digital. After the opening synthesizers, the first thing you hear is something that sounds like a bird calling out into the horizon, before the horns come in, followed by those banging 808 drums. You can hear other drums too, quieter ones like tablas from south Asia, or hand drums from west Africa. And then you get something that sounds like a marimba, or xylophone. Put it all together and it sounds like the world – the musical world – with the old dancing away with the new. Dream-like. 'Pacific State' flies around with soaring notes and a searching kind of melody. It sounds hopeful but calm, despite the pounding drum. It sounds free.

Most importantly, house music is all about freedom and unity. Freedom from the barriers and conflicts that separate us, and unity as one people, together. House was always focused on collective uplift, creating bonds between different groups – especially those treated like outsiders. I've already mentioned that house was created by black Americans. It welcomed black people, but also people of Latino heritage, as well as gay communities who were openly discriminated against by mainstream society. Here, we see the dance floor becoming a location of togetherness: an ideal that the world is still struggling to reach.

'Nothing Compares 2 U'

Sinéad O'Connor (1990)

Question: Does pain live forever?

If you watch the video to this song, you'll see mainly one thing. Sinéad O'Connor's face, in close up, singing the song while looking at you directly down the lens of the camera. It's very hard to look away. As she sings, she goes through a whole range of emotions, struggling, in real time, to cope with the power and truth of her words. Towards the end of the video, two tears fall down her face, as she is seemingly overwhelmed by the emotional power of the song.

When millions of people heard Sinéad sing this song, and saw her in this video, they were moved. It's a reaction that still stands today, born out of the simplicity of raw emotion. You can not only see and hear but also feel the belief in her words, talking about how hard it is to be without someone you love.

Loss and pain are two of the strongest emotions you can feel; everyone knows this. As a popular music artist, Sinéad O'Connor has often dealt with these feelings, pouring them into her work. She has said that the song is an 'eternal tribute' to her mother, who died when Sinéad was only a teenager. That's where the tears come from in the video – they're real. For Sinéad, the song is a conversation with her lost mother.

As we have seen elsewhere in this book, and we shall definitely see again, with pain often comes struggle. The pain of racial injustice fuelled the struggle of the civil rights movement back in the 1960s. In the 1970s, the pain of senseless conflict led to protest songs against the Vietnam War. And here, *personal* pain is turning into the struggle to carry on. This is one of the things that humans can do: find ways of carrying on when times are hard.

Much of Sinéad's life has been devoted to fighting against injustices. One famous example is shortly after the release of 'Nothing Compares 2 U' when she was performing live on a big TV show in America. At one point, she took out a picture of Pope John Paul II, who was at that time the head of the Catholic Church. She proceeded to rip the picture into pieces. Why? It was a political statement. For Sinéad, it was a protest against sexual abuse within the church. She felt strongly about the evil of children being abused and made a point of showing the world how much it angered her, in a very shocking way. As someone who was raised as Catholic myself, I know how much respect the Pope holds as the figurehead of the whole church. Sinéad O'Connor really was looking to make everyone pay attention.

Her actions drew a lot of criticism from people all over the world, including other celebrities. Madonna, one of the biggest pop stars of all time, openly questioned the action, asking why Sinéad would target someone who so many people look up to. Years later, Sinéad would go on to write a letter to a younger pop artist called Miley Cyrus, asking her to think about the sexualisation of young women in pop music and highlighting sexism in modern society.

These actions are, of course, controversial, meaning

that many people agreed, and many did not. You could see this up close at a tribute concert to Bob Dylan in 1992, where Sinéad O'Connor was met with a combination of both cheers and boos from the assembled crowd, leaving her having to shout her performance over the noise.

Whether you agree with her actions or not, it's clear that Sinéad O'Connor has taken a stand against injustices as she sees them, and perhaps the take-away message is simple: live out your beliefs and speak out against injustice against others. You might get it wrong, and it's not always easy, but trying to make the world better is a lot of what the artists in this book (and a lot of artists in history – not just in music) have tried to do.

Something you can't see in the 'Nothing Compares 2 U' video, and something that Sinéad herself wouldn't have known, is just how turbulent her life would become. As story goes, she even got into an argument with Prince, the artist who originally wrote 'Nothing Compares 2 U', after he told her to stop swearing in interviews. Can you imagine?

Decades later, she changed her name not once, but twice, as she went on a personal journey of finding her own identity. The first name change (to Magda Davitt) was intended to distance her from problems of the past, linked to names of old. The second (where she changed her name to Shuhada' Sadaqat) was to embrace the religion of Islam, which she decided was the best path to follow spiritually.

In 2022, when I was researching this book, Magda Davitt suffered an unspeakable bereavement. Her seventeen-year-old son died in early January that year. Thirty-two years after she cried for her mother, she would be forced to cry for her son. I watched 'Nothing Compares 2 U', and I felt like crying too.

It's worth remembering that all the musicians in this book are real people, with real struggles, tragedies and pain. It's amazing how music can bring us together, even when musicians themselves do things that can divide our opinions. Speaking out for justice isn't always easy. And it can make your life far more difficult. I dedicate this chapter to anyone who has ever tried to make things better.

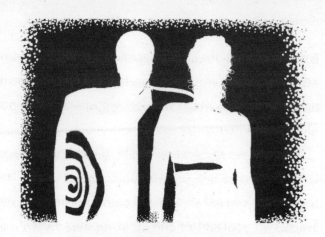

'7 Seconds'

Neneh Cherry and Youssou N'Dour (1994)

Question: How big is the musical world?

I've checked. There aren't many songs out there that are performed in *three* different languages. It might even be a bit unusual, considering the fact that most songs are made by individuals or groups from one place, at one time.

But the world doesn't speak one single language. At the last count, there are currently somewhere near

6,500 separate languages spoken by humans on this planet called Earth. As a species, we are varied and diverse, with all sorts of ways of communicating based on where we end up. It's a wondrous and beautiful thing.

In the song '7 Seconds' you'll hear three different languages. The first is a language called Wolof, from Senegal in west Africa. Wolof is one of the most popular languages spoken in Senegal, sung here by Youssou N'Dour, who is from Senegal himself. When I first heard this song, as a teenager in the 1990s, I didn't know this. But music being what it is, I could still enjoy the song and feel a connection to the lyrics I didn't understand, which we shall come back to later.

The next language you'll hear is English. You'll probably be familiar with this one, as it is currently spoken by somewhere near 1.5 billion people worldwide. This has a lot to do with the historic power of the British Empire, which at one point, just before the First World War, controlled nearly a quarter of people on the planet. It's no accident that so many people have grown up speaking the language of the British Empire, because the empire was so powerful, for so long. Interestingly enough, fewer than half a billion people currently list English as their first language, which means that most English speakers are not English or British.

In '7 Seconds' the English parts are sung by Neneh Cherry, who you might remember from the song 'Buffalo Stance' in *Musical Truth*. Neneh Cherry is British but, like so many of us, she also represents a diverse mix of cultures, places and heritages: London, New York, Sweden (where she was born) and Sierra Leone (where her biological father is from), to name a few.

The third and final language you'll hear in '7 Seconds' is French. French is the language of France, but it is also spoken thirty-eight other countries, many of which list French as the official language. This goes all the way back to the colonial era of the eighteenth and nineteenth centuries, when powerful European nations (like France and Britain) went all over the world taking control of other countries. One of these countries was Senegal, which explains why Youssou N'Dour sings in both Wolof and French.

What makes all of this fascinating is that it's all made up. Languages, all 6,500 of them, are the creations of people. We aren't born with any sense of languages or the countries that they are attached to. It's why you can take a baby from anywhere, raise them anywhere else, and they will instinctively learn the language around them, given time.

This is what '7 Seconds' is all about. It's a song that

asks you to think about those first few seconds of a person's life, when they are a baby with no knowledge of the outside world, at all. No language, no nation, no race, no colour, no history. As Neneh Cherry sings at one point: when a child is born, it has no concept of the tone of skin it's living in. Then, as Youssou N'Dour sings later on: there are a million voices telling that child what to think and who to be. It happens to all of us, but in those first few seconds, we are . . . clear.

I know. It's a difficult idea to grapple with. The first verse, in Wolof, wrestles with the idea that we are not always what people see us as. That people might see us as our skin colour, or our ethnicity, or our language, but this is not the limit of who we are and who we can be. Later, in French, Youssou asks us to think about forgetting about colour, saying that there are too many views on race that complicate how we treat each other. If you flick back through this book, you'll see that he's right. Race and racism have been a complication for humanity, often leading to conflict, hurt, injustice and suffering.

I can't help but return to my own thoughts about this song, back in 1994, when I was twelve. It was something I had never heard before, full of sounds that sounded distant and wistful, like a traveller going

157

on a long journey with no destination. It washed over me, in a good way, with Neneh's and Youssou's voices intermingling beautifully, in different languages. It was an example of how popular music could travel outside of what you already knew, bringing you closer to things you were far apart from.

'7 Seconds' is all about what brings humans together and the innocence we all have as newborn babies. Remember, it was written at a time when apartheid in South Africa was just coming to an end, a period of separation and segregation along racial lines. Maybe this is part of the reason why the song was so successful – who knows? In any case, it stands proud as an example of how beautiful we can be, together, when we rise above our differences.

'Wannabe'

Spice Girls (1996)

Question: What do you really, really want?

I'll never forget it.

When I was growing up in the 1990s, there was a music programme on the television called *Top of the Pops*. It had been on TV for as long as I remember, coming on once a week to show you all the new songs and reveal who was where in the pop music charts. This was back when people really cared a lot about what was number one. And apart from the radio, it was the only place to hear new pop songs (without buying them on compact discs or cassette tapes).

One week, a new group performed live on *Top of the Pops*. They were called the Spice Girls: a group of five women from different parts of the UK. The Spice Girls were a 'girl group', a female equivalent to 'boy bands', which also usually contained five members and sang love songs that were supposed to make teenage girls go crazy.

The Spice Girls were something different. The song they performed was called 'Wannabe' and it was like nothing we had ever seen before. It was loud and funky, and full of personality, with each singer having their own section to introduce themselves to the world. It was fun and fresh and completely addictive – everything you would want from a great pop song. It even had a rap near the middle, which caught my attention because of how much I loved hip-hop.

Seemingly overnight, the whole world seemed to be talking about the Spice Girls. Who were they? Where did they come from? And why did they have such strange nicknames? I'll list them:

- Victoria Adams – 'Posh Spice'
- Melanie Brown – 'Scary Spice'

- Emma Bunton – 'Baby Spice'
- Melanie Chisolm – 'Sporty Spice'
- Geri Halliwell – 'Ginger Spice'

A lot of people thought that all this was just a bit of silly fun. They were a group who had been put together for the pop charts, rather than growing up as close friends. The nicknames seemed almost childish, like silly insults, and the song itself didn't seem to have any deep or serious meaning. But as we have seen (and will see again) pop music doesn't always have to be clever to be profound.

'Wannabe' felt like a moment of change. The first time the Spice Girls had ever been seen was for the launch of a new TV channel – Channel 5. It was a big moment for the group, and helped 'Wannabe' become a huge hit. But much more than that, 'Wannabe' became the soundtrack to a new appreciation of female empowerment. I didn't have the words for it back then, but this song was helping to usher in a new wave of feminism for the late twentieth century. Suddenly, the phrase 'girl power' was being used everywhere. The Spice Girls were symbols of strong, empowered women, finding strength and friendship in their unity and confidence. As the lyrics even say, *friendship never ends*.

In a way, I'm breaking the rules of enjoying popular music by writing a book like this. I'm not sure if pop songs are meant to be analysed and turned into clever-sounding essays. However, we can't ignore the fact that sexism was still huge social problem in the world in the 1990s, just as it continues to be today. As the Spice Girls were breaking the charts, Britain had still only ever had one female prime minister and women were still suffering from deep inequality at all levels of society. The Spice Girls didn't invent girl power (it was a phrase that was first used by punk musicians in the early 1990s) but they brought it to the world in a way that no one could ignore.

After the Spice Girls, there was a whole new conversation around feminism, inspiring a generation of girls, and boys, who were ready to challenge and fight sexism, while singing along to crazy lyrics about slamming your body down and zigazig-ah, whatever that means.

In the years that followed the huge success of 'Wannabe', the world of entertainment started to see figures of female empowerment in all sorts of areas. Disney films began to feature heroic female leads like *Mulan* (1998) while a vampire-killing cheerleader called Buffy became a sci-fi superstar on TV. It seems obvious to say now, but the world I grew up in needed to see that girls and women could be as impressive and confident as boys and men. The history of feminism stretches far and wide across history, with huge feminist movements from the nineteenth century and beyond, known as waves:

- The first wave: Took place in the late nineteenth century and asked for women (in the West) to be given specific rights, including the right to vote in elections.
- The second wave: Took place during the 1960s and 1970s, focusing on the deeper reasons why women are oppressed in the first place. This wave of feminism also looked to challenge society by coming up with new ideas over what women should be allowed to do.
- The third wave: Took place towards the end of the twentieth century, into the 1990s. Encouraged new freedoms among women and girls, with a big focus on the choice to be whatever you wanted to be. This wave also started to look more carefully at the different experiences of women who aren't white,

examining the intersections (overlaps) of racism and sexism.

In a way, the Spice Girls are a part of this ongoing story.

I can't lie: I'm pleased that so many of the artists in this book are female. The music industry, like so much of society in general, can be an incredibly sexist place. This is something that I was not invited to think about much when I was growing up. I was lucky enough to grow up with two older sisters who always led the way, giving me positive female role models for as long as I can remember. All of this means that I can recognise the importance of moments like this one, when the Spice Girls brought girl power, and third wave feminist ideas, into the mainstream. Take a moment to celebrate what they helped to create with a song that stands proud in modern feminist history.

'Brimful of Asha'

Cornershop (1997)

Question: How does Indian music teach us about the world of power?

When 'Brimful of Asha' was first released, it was part of something called 'Britpop', a new type of music from young, cool, British bands in the 1990s.

Cornershop was a Britpop band, and their name let you know that they had strong Indian influences. One of the stereotypes about Indian people in Britain is that they often own convenience shops on the corner of local streets, known as corner shops. So when two brothers with Indian heritage formed a new band with some friends, *Cornershop* was a good way of nodding to Indian culture.

British Indians have suffered from racist discrimination and prejudice for as long as Britain has had a relationship with India. It was only in 1947 that India became independent of British rule, after which there was an increase in Indian people travelling to live and work in Britain.

Despite the fact that the links between Britain and India go back hundreds of years (as we shall explore later), Indian communities in Britain were often met with anger, hatred and bigotry. Britain took direct control over India all the way back in the 1850s, creating a see-saw of power that was never fair or balanced. For modern people of Indian heritage, this comes with a history of exploitation, prejudice, discrimination and racism.

One way of responding to such treatment is to rise above it by asserting your cultural identity. Rather than hide, or try to change, you can be deliberately proud of your heritage. In 1991, when the band Cornershop was formed by the brothers Tjinder and Avtar Singh, along with friends Ben Ayres and David Chambers, anti-Indian racism was commonplace. Since the end of the Second World War, non-white British people had been the target of racist groups (such as the National Front and the British National Party) who never wanted Britain to welcome ethnic minorities. For ordinary people in minority communities, this meant a life of fear and unwanted conflict. Growing up in the 1990s, I saw and heard racism against ethnic minority communities, including those from Indian and Pakistani heritage. There were cruel jokes repeated on TV, in homes, workplaces and playgrounds, and a general belief that it was OK to laugh at people who were 'different' from the majority.

In this environment, any music from a minority culture will automatically do two things:

- Celebrate the minority culture.
- Empower members of the minority community.

'Brimful of Asha' did exactly this. It was a song that made India seem cool, right at the cutting edge of modern Britpop music.

When I first heard 'Brimful of Asha', I sang along happily to the catchy tune but, like a lot of people, I had no idea what most of it meant. I had no idea that 'Asha' was a reference to Asha Bhosle, a legendary singer in Indian cinema who has recorded more than 12,000 songs, a world record. At one point, Tjinder calls Asha Bhosle *sadi rani*, which means *our queen* in Punjabi (an Indian and Pakistani language). I didn't know that 'Asha' also translates as 'hope'. I didn't know anything about Lata Mangeshkar, another legendary film singer who is also Asha Bosle's sister. I didn't know about Mohammed Rafi, Solid State Radio, Jacques Dutronc, All India Radio, Non Public, or Trojan Records ... But now, with a bit of research, I've discovered that these are all references to popular music in different parts of the world. This song is a celebration of music, modern music, and the ways that music can feel like a warm hug from a loving parent.

This is clearly a song with deep meanings and lots to learn about Indian culture and history. It challenges the Indian government and says that the love of singing and cinema is stronger than rules and regulations set out by the people who run the country. That's why there's a line about not caring about government warnings. But it's also full of nostalgia and fond memories of India's recent past, taking us into the world of Indian cinema known as *Bollywood* (which we're going to meet again in twelve years and eleven pages' time, when a huge song from a hit movie will shed even more light on India's relationship with Britain).

Any song that allows you to see more of a particular culture, or the history of a particular group of people, is an important song. In 1997 'Brimful of Asha' did exactly this, in a country that has struggled to be inclusive towards its marginalised groups.

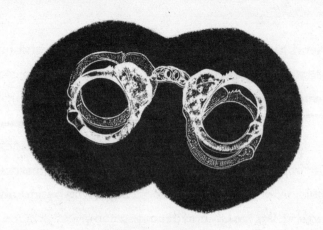

'Cry'

Swiss (2005)

Question: When does music turn into grief?

Sometimes, it can all feel like too much.

Sometimes, the weight of the world feels like too much to bear, and all you can do is hold your head in your hands and wonder why. It's uncomfortable, and most of us would rather not think about it too much, but the kind of problems that the world can throw at you can lead to real pain.

For musicians, this can be a powerful feeling. It can

lead to outpourings of grief and confusion and hurt that turn into profound pieces of art, where the meeting point between creativity and hurt becomes something that can stir your soul.

In 2005, young black people living in Britain had a lot to think about. For these communities (many of which had grandparents and parents who weren't born in Britain), the UK had become a complicated place to call home. It was only after the Second World War, in 1945, that large numbers of people from the Caribbean started to arrive in Britain, coming to the so-called 'Mother Country', as it was known under the British Empire. Later, in the 1970s, we saw groups arriving from African countries that had also been colonised by Britain, including Ghana (previously called the 'Gold Coast'), where my parents were born.

Even though they had every reason to consider Britain their home, these optimistic new arrivals were very often met with hostility and racism. It wasn't only verbal and physical racist abuse, being told to 'go back home' and shown that they were not welcome. It also meant a whole system of inequality that meant that black British people didn't have access to adequate housing or job opportunities.

Social deprivation has been a key part of the black

British experience. Right up until today, black families are more likely than many other groups to live in poverty, and the system that creates this reality is at fault.

The 1980s saw tensions reach a boiling point, with protests against the authorities, escalating into full-blown uprisings, described as riots, in parts of the country where black communities had gathered. A lot of this came from interactions with the police, which unfairly targeted black people. For decades, black people suffered suspicion, discrimination and abuse at the hands of the people who were supposed to protect them.

By the end of the 1990s, it was confirmed in a huge independent report that London's Metropolitan Police Service (the biggest police force in the country) was *institutionally racist*. The report, led by someone called Sir William Macpherson, came after the murder of a black teenager called Stephen Lawrence, killed in a racist attack in London in 1993. Stephen's murder was a tragedy which revealed some blinding truths. It showed that racism was alive in modern British society and it also proved that the criminal justice system was failing to do its job, forcing Stephen's family to become campaigners. His mother, Doreen Lawrence, has since become a baroness due to her unending work to make things better. Right now, only two of Stephen's killers have been found guilty of their crime.

In 2005, a young rapper called Swiss would have been well aware of these problems. Like so many of us who have grown up black in Britain, he would have known all about the struggles with racism that make life difficult, the racism you can see and hear and the racism deep within the structures that society is made from. He would have had friends and family who had suffered from poverty and discrimination, or gone to school with people who were pushed out of the system because of long histories of conflict and mistrust.

'Cry' is all about these harsh realities. It's a raw and honest song about all the unfairness in the world that young black people growing up in the millennium were facing. There's so much in here. He talks about the violence and criminality that can seep into areas of urban deprivation where people are 'broke' – made poor by a system that doesn't seek to empower underprivileged communities. He talks about how life became risky after he started to see initial success through music and the desperation he and his friends felt to protect themselves. He talks about actual prisons and the mental chains of not believing in hope, which can make areas of poverty feel like prisons too. He talks about the failure of the government to protect us and a system that makes violent weapons available in the first place. He talks about racism going back to transatlantic slavery, where black Africans were abused and exploited by white Europeans. He talks about how black people haven't been taught the whole truth of history at school. He talks about the senseless waste of life that comes from urban violence, listing old friends who didn't make it. He talks about the futility of drug use, and how people use drugs to try to escape reality. He talks about Stephen Lawrence and everything we should have learned from that moment of national shame. There's deep vulnerability in here. His voice strains with emotion as he tells you all about the pain of struggle and loss. 'Cry' feels like a diary entry from a period of history that Britain needs to examine. It's personal, but it also invites you to really feel the injustices of racism in modern Britain.

And in all of this, Swiss talks about having to be strong, with a responsibility to look after your family and survive against the odds, getting up when you fall down and feeling scared all the time. This is a song that shows that there can be a kind of power that comes out of feeling powerless. One example of this happened in September 2022, when a twenty-three-year-old man from London, a rapper just like Swiss, was shot dead by the police. His name is Chris Kaba, and he lived in a place called Streatham, near where other famous British rappers such as Stormzy and Dave grew up. The murder of Chris Kaba brought immense pain and suffering to his family and the wider black community. It was an awful reminder of how racism was still alive in British society, with the institution that is supposed to protect us continuing to threaten our safety. Within one week of his death, a huge march took place in London, attended by thousands of people who wanted answers – people ready to shout, chant and cry, for justice. Writing this book at the time, I thought about how much society had to learn, and how suffering can open a door to meaningful change.

This chapter is dedicated to the legacy of Chris Kaba and everyone seeking justice against racism in the UK.

'Jai Ho'

A. R. Rahman (2009)

Question: Who gets to decide the winners?

As I've mentioned earlier, India and Britain have a very long and very complicated historical relationship with each other.

The story begins right at the end of the year 1600, when a company was created in England with the intention of making trade links with India and parts of east and south-east Asia. The East India Company became massively powerful, trading things like sugar, spices, tea, cotton and silk well into the nineteenth century.

As a result, the East India Company ended up ruling over huge parts of India. All this changed in 1858, when Britain took direct control of India after an Indian rebellion against the East India Company.

So, for the next eighty-nine years, India was controlled by Britain as part of the British Empire. It was a complex and often difficult time. India was still incredibly valuable to Britain because of rare items such as spices and jewels. Beyond this, India had a large population. Many Indian people were drafted into the British army and, as a result, Indian soldiers became a key part of Britain's military power.

It wouldn't be until 1947 that India would become independent of British rule. But that doesn't mean that the two countries went their separate ways. Multiple generations of Indian people had grown up with Britain as their colonial leaders. Also, Britain had encouraged conflict between different religious groups in India, as a way of keeping control. After 1947, Britain saw a big jump in the number of Indians migrating to the UK. A big part of this was the British Nationality Act of 1948. This was a piece of legislation that invited anyone from the Commonwealth to come and live and work in the

UK (at a time when Britain desperately needed workers to help rebuild the country after the Second World War).

Meanwhile, back in India, a decision had been made by the British government that would have a devastating impact upon the lives of millions of ordinary people. It was called *the partition*, and it was the division of British India into two countries: India and Pakistan. The results of this partition were brutal. Up to twenty million people found themselves homeless, while religious conflicts led to unspeakable violence and hundreds of thousands of deaths. This is what happens when big decisions are made about whole countries without care being taken over the people affected. This is what happens when countries are allowed to rule over other countries, instead of working together as equals. This is what happens when you have greed and insensitivity, for hundreds of years.

After the Nationality Act, new arrivals to the UK often faced open hostility, prejudice and racism. By 1961, there were over 100,000 people from India and Pakistan in the UK, up from only 43,000 in 1951. These communities began to have a lasting impact on British culture. This is maybe most clearly seen in the popularity of Indian food. (You'll struggle to find any British person who hasn't heard of curry, for instance.)

Modern India has matured into a global power in its own right. It has the largest population of any country in the world, complete with several cities of over 10 million people. Like many modern nations, India contains outrageous wealth and stark poverty all at the same time. India also has one of the fastest-growing economies on the planet, which means that it is making money quicker than many other countries, in lots of different ways. One of the most famous industries in India is the film industry, known as *Bollywood*, based in the city of Mumbai. It's huge. In 2020, the Bollywood film industry was worth somewhere near 183 billion Indian rupees (a *lot* of money) and regularly churns out hundreds of films loved by millions.

A big part of the Bollywood movie experience is music. Many Bollywood films are essentially musicals, fuelled by massive musical numbers complete with choreography and energetic dancers. These movies are a full-on cinematic experience, an explosion of sound and colour that celebrates traditional Indian culture with confidence and style. This is the power of music, culture and art: way more than simple entertainment, they can be a source of genuine empowerment too.

Allah Rakha Rahman is a seriously successful composer and producer making music for Indian films.

His work is so celebrated and respected that he has won over forty awards, including a special award from the Indian government.

In 2008, Rahman worked on the music for a film called *Slumdog Millionaire*. It was a huge release. It was a British film with a British director called Danny Boyle, and it starred Dev Patel, a British actor of Indian heritage. Let's think about that for second. Here, we're looking at a film that's taking on the power of the Hollywood film industry, led by British creatives. It stars a child of migrants to Britain who were originally from Indian communities in Kenya (that's where Dev Patel's parents were born) who met in London. The film itself is all about a teenage boy living in the slums of Mumbai, seeking to make his fortune via a TV game show that was invented in Britain. And the whole thing ends with a song, 'Jai Ho', written by a superstar Indian musician.

History is never straightforward, is it? The histories of different countries cross and intertwine in all sorts of ways, leading to unpredictable surprises along the way. Sometimes, it can be tempting to look at history as a series of winners and losers, but this isn't how it works. When you look at India and Britain, it makes more sense to look at history as a series of meeting points, moments of interaction that change the direction of travel.

'Jai Ho' roughly translates to a phrase meaning 'let there be victory'. It's an optimistic feeling that we all need to give us hope for the future – the hope that we will succeed. Through history, different countries have had very different fates, but hope for the future is common to every nation. It's why every country still stands up to sing their national anthem.

Slumdog Millionaire is an example of how hope can turn into celebration. The film won eight Academy Awards (Oscars) out of the ten that it was nominated for, including Best Picture and Best Original Song, for 'Jai Ho'.

It wasn't all happy times though. Many people believe that the film doesn't show poverty in India in a realistic or fair way, while others think that it celebrates Western culture more than Indian culture. There are no easy answers here. Just like we have seen in the historical relationship between India and Britain, there can be complications and conflict when different cultures exist together. Thankfully, these differences can also come together to make moments of beauty and power. All it needs is enough space, truth, honesty and respect to let every culture shine.

'Waka Waka (This Time for Africa)'

Shakira (2010)

Question: Can the whole world ever celebrate as one?

Sorry. We're back to football.

Actually, I take that back. Not sorry at all. You can't avoid it. Not only is it the biggest sport in human history, but every four years we get a huge international footballing event that invites every country in the world to a massive competition, to see who's the best at kicking a small ball into a big net.

2010 was a World Cup year. It was the nineteenth World Cup and as usual, the whole world seemed to be bristling with excitement to see who would come out on top. One of the things that was different about this World Cup was that it was held in the continent of Africa, for the first time in World Cup history. The host nation was South Africa, who had won the chance to do so out of a selection of African nations.

As someone of African heritage myself, this felt like a big deal. It was a reminder that Africa was in the process of redefining itself on the global stage, with modern African countries emerging as places that could compete with any other country. For years while I was growing up, Africa was often depicted as a place of poverty and need, with exotic animals to look at and not much else. Nothing could be further from the truth. As a continent, it's full of countries with a rich tapestry of histories and cultures. It has gleaming megacities and ancient traditions, hundreds of languages, pioneering industries and more, spanning over fifty different countries. It's crazy to think that even now, many people still think of Africa as one place, despite how multilayered and varied it actually is.

Many people love Shakira's 'Waka Waka' (over

three *billion* views and counting on YouTube) and some people dislike it. Some people find it inspiring while others think it its nonsensical and silly. Some praise its optimistic spirit, but others criticise it for having a lead singer who is not from an African country. (Shakira is Colombian. She is thought to have been inspired to write 'Waka Waka' by a song from 1986 called 'Zangaléwa', recorded by Golden Sounds, a band from Cameroon.)

No matter how you look at it, 'Waka Waka' is definitely intended to be a celebration of Africa. The World Cup has a way of putting different countries under the spotlight, and in 2010, it wasn't just South Africa but the entire African continent that was being focused on. The song makes it clear that we are supposed to be celebrating Africa as a whole, while also enjoying friendly competition of international football, and when you look at world history over centuries, that's important.

Since as far back as the nineteenth century, Africa has been on the receiving end of awful treatment from European countries seeking to establish their wealth and power on the world stage. Throughout the 1800s there was something called the 'Scramble for Africa', whereby European nations tried to get all the most valuable resources out of Africa, for their own gain. Precious metals, natural oil and fuel, valuable crops like cocoa and coffee, and much more. Then, after years of scrambling, leading nations sat down to carve up the continent and decide who got what. As I mentioned way back on page 17 the part of west Africa that my parents come from (now called Ghana), was rich in gold, so Britain named it the Gold Coast after colonising the region. It makes me wonder a few things . . .

What if Britain had never colonised the 'Gold Coast' and I was born and raised in that part of west Africa, rather than England?

What if Africa had never been colonised and exploited by European nations? Would an African nation have hosted the World Cup before 2010?

What if the vision for a united African super-state had come true, in a United States of Africa? Would anyone be able to defeat their football team?

What if African people had not been enslaved for the benefit of other countries? Would racism have ever even had a chance to flourish in the way that it has?

It's interesting that despite all this happiness and optimism, conflict is never too far away. The lyrics to 'Waka Waka' compare footballers to soldiers on a battlefield. It's a fair comparison, and a simple piece of poetry, but it's also a reminder of how fighting is so often part of the human experience, especially when people meet differences. One of the most famous African leaders of all time is Kwame Nkrumah, the first president of Ghana after the country won its independence in 1957. Ghana was one of the first African nations to become independent of the British Empire. Nkrumah had a vision for all of Africa to be liberated in this way and then unite as one. When I visited Ghana in 2009 I picked up a copy of his book *Africa Must Unite*, and it gave me a whole new perspective on what Africa could have been, or might one day become. The problem is that these kinds of changes are like trying to change the tides, or switch off gravity.

> *'Unite we must . . . We must unite in order to achieve the full liberation of our continent.'*
> —KWAME NKRUMAH

In his lifetime, Nkrumah was unsuccessful in his aims, but his vision has been shared by many others over the years. Frustratingly, many African countries are still often treated as 'developing' nations, lacking the influence and power of their global counterparts. In 2010 'Waka Waka' asked us to think about how this time was for Africa. A football tournament is one thing, but when will it really be Africa's time? And what might that ultimately look like?

'Work'

Rihanna featuring Drake (2016)

Question: How big can a 'small' country become?

The closest thing to a royal family in the USA is celebrities. As far as modern countries go, the United States of America is not very old at all, created in the 1770s as a breakaway colony of Britain. The formation of the USA came at the expense of Native American communities who were already on American soil long before the continent was 'discovered' by European explorers. From this point onwards, the identity of the

USA has been linked with suffering rooted in white European power, starting with the violent colonisation of North American territories.

Now, many of the most famous people on the planet have come from America, often from the worlds of sport and entertainment, including film stars and, of course, musicians.

The influence of American culture on the world has been huge, especially in the twentieth century. As a result, this book is full of American stars. As we've seen, the twentieth century saw an explosion of musical styles that have spread in popularity all over the world. Jazz, R & B, soul, rock, disco and hip-hop to name a few. It's why still, to this day, so many of us look to the United States to see the biggest stars in the entertainment galaxy. For decades, America has produced famous men and women who catch our attention and dazzle us with their shine. The US music industry has grown so big and successful that it continuously churns out famous recording artists. This is one of the reasons that it's so hard to write a book like this one without focusing on American musicians.

It also shows that black America is central to global popular culture, which in turn means that black American stars are often like royalty. We've seen some of the biggest examples already, including Michael Jackson, known as the King of Pop, and Aretha Franklin, known as the Queen of Soul. By 2016, there were many more to list, and Rihanna was definitely on a throne of her own.

You might have heard the phrase 'so and so put so and so *on the map*'. It's an old phrase used when someone makes the place they are from famous, by being successful. Rihanna lives in America, but you could say that she put Barbados 'on the map' in this way.

Rihanna (full name: Robyn Rihanna Fenty) is originally from Barbados, one of the Caribbean islands. With hundreds of millions of records sold worldwide, she is one of the biggest artists in history, having risen to fame in the US in the early 2000s. One of the things that makes her special is the fact she represents her Bajan roots so strongly. Her music can be categorised as modern R & B, a popular black American genre, but she also incorporates Caribbean influences that have become increasingly popular.

'Work' is an example of this. It's a beautifully cool song with a pulsing, swaying rhythm that fully sounds like it's from the islands. Remember the birth of the 'riddim' in 1985's 'Under Mi Sleng Teng'? Well, here we have a riddim catapulted into the brightest of spotlights. The name of the riddim that is sampled in 'Work' is from a 1999 song called 'Sail Away' by a Jamaican artist called Richie Stephens. The 'Sail Away' riddim was then used by many different popular dancehall artists including Sean Paul, Beenie Man and Mr Vegas. I love how riddims are shared and used by artists in the same genre. In an age of popularity, competition and music moneymaking, there's something refreshing and friendly about one piece of music being passed around so freely.

Music from the Caribbean was always popular where I grew up, in Brixton, a part of London with a strong Caribbean community. I heard the sounds of reggae, dancehall, soca and ska as part of my childhood. As I got older, I noticed that reggae in particular was becoming popular in the mainstream British charts, probably because of the black British community. But I never thought that the USA would ever lean towards the Caribbean musically in the way that it did after the millennium. Suddenly, it wasn't unusual to see and hear US megastars such as Drake, Beyoncé and Justin Bieber making songs that sound like the songs I heard in 1980s black Britain.

Historically, Barbados has not been as economically or globally powerful as the USA. Barbados was colonised by England in 1625 (long before the USA was created) and exploited as a place where enslaved

Africans were forced to grow crops to be sold for profit. In 1661, the Barbados Slave Code made it legal for people to be made into slaves because of the colour of their skin. This built racism into the law.

In 1774, when the USA won its independence from Britain, Barbados was still under British rule, with the head of the British monarchy residing as the Bajan head of state. While the USA was busy setting itself up as a (white) global power, Barbados was still very much in the shadows of imperial rule.

It wasn't until 2021 that Barbados elected its first president, a lawyer called Sandra Mason. President Mason replaced the Queen of England as the Bajan head of state. Barbados was finally a republic – free of British rule.

Rihanna is as important to the political world as she is to the worlds of music and entertainment. In 2018, the government of Barbados appointed her as an official ambassador of the country in recognition of her success and her charity work, having helped various groups including women, cancer patients, vulnerable children and the victims of natural disasters. She is also a hugely successful business leader, having launched Fenty Beauty – a cosmetics range designed for a range of skin tones, named after Rihanna's last name. And then, on the first day of Barbados being a republic (30 November 2021), Rihanna was declared a national hero. All this from a so-called pop star.

This book is about *politics, power and popular music*. I think there really is something powerful about songs from small places that go on to do big things. 'Work' falls into this category. It's a milestone in Rihanna's career that leans heavily upon Caribbean culture (in a genre that was dominated by men when I was growing up). It's worth mentioning that 'Work' also features the vocals of Drake, who really is one of the biggest superstars of all time – a rapper and singer from Canada who conquered the entertainment world in the 2010s. Drake himself has become increasingly interested in Caribbean culture, sometimes even speaking in the patois I heard when I was growing up around Caribbean communities in south London in the 1980s and 1990s. It's safe to say that the Caribbean is a major part of the pop music puzzle – something that was helped along by Rihanna's dancehall hit.

'Old Town Road'

Lil Nas X (2019)

Question: What is the future of masculinity in pop music?

'Toxic masculinity' is a phrase that didn't exist when I was at school growing up. It refers to a set of rules, sort of, for how to be a man, but these rules are actually damaging to men and boys. Toxic masculinity says that men and boys should be tough and strong, never weak or vulnerable – even though being vulnerable is part of being a human being. It says that being violent and aggressive is a good thing if it gives you power.

It also sees masculinity as being naturally better than femininity, which means that boys are seen as better than girls. This is called misogyny, which means disliking women.

Another part of toxic masculinity is the belief that real men are always heterosexual, or 'straight', meaning that toxic masculinity does not trust or like gay people. This is homophobia, a type of discrimination that is common across different societies all over the world.

One common criticism of hip-hop is that it contains toxic masculinity. Rap music often features men acting tough and talking about how powerful they are. Rappers are often hypermasculine, which means that they act like over-the-top, manly cartoon characters – big muscles, aggressive behaviour, showing off and being irresistible to women. That said, it's never fair to blame hip-hop for a social problem that is much bigger than it is. Toxic masculinity, misogyny and homophobia exist in all avenues of life and society.

One thing you might have noticed about society is that there don't seem to be many gay men in certain areas of sport, entertainment, business and politics. This is where homophobia comes into it, where society makes it difficult for gay people to have equal opportunities, so much so that some gay people might even hide their sexuality from the world. Hip-hop is no exception. In all my years of being a fan of hip-hop, I'd never once seen or heard of an openly gay rapper. It just seemed to go against the rules; rappers were simply not allowed to be gay.

This all changed in 2018, when a teenager called Montero Lamar Hill decided to make a song called 'Old Town Road'.

'Old Town Road' is not about being gay. It's a song that fuses the two genres of hip-hop and country into a fantastic blend of originality. It's a bouncy, laid-back song with pounding, electronic hip-hop drums that lilt along like a cowboy on a lazy horse. Traditionally, country music is very white, while hip-hop music is very black, making a combination of the two a bit of a cultural surprise. But it works, proving that things that you might not think should go together can go together very well indeed. 'Old Town Road' is so much fun that it quickly went viral, being shared by millions of people on the internet, particularly the social media app TikTok. And amazingly, it's a song that Montero made at home, living with his sister after deciding to leave school. He found the instrumental for sale online and bought it for $30.

The song blew up. By the end of 2019 it had sold

more than ten million copies in the USA alone, and Montero had even recorded a new version with a country music superstar called Billy Ray Cyrus. It was official: Montero was a star.

It was while 'Old Town Road' was climbing the charts that Montero decided to tell the world he was gay. He wasn't sure if his fans would stay loyal to him, because of the homophobia that is so common in society. This is a sad thing to admit, that even this far into the twenty-first century, a young musician felt worried about his sexuality. He knew that being gay would make it hard for him to be accepted in the worlds of hip-hop and country, and in the world at large.

Montero the musician was now Lil Nas X the gay rapper, and here's the thing: his sexuality didn't hold him back. Yes, he was bullied and criticised by small-minded people who can't see how cruel and stupid homophobia is, but he also drew support from many others who celebrated what he represents: the freedom to be yourself and a future without homophobia at all. 'Old Town Road' was the start of a dazzling career for Lil Nas X. He continues to make music and express himself creatively, rather than hiding away from his haters.

It's worth noting that Lil Nas X came out on Twitter on the last day of Pride Month in the USA. Pride Month is a month dedicated to celebrating LGBTQ+ communities. It also remembers a series of uprisings that took place in New York City back in 1969, when groups of young gay people fought back against the police at a bar called the Stonewall Inn. These 'Stonewall Riots' are recognised as a key moment in the history of gay rights.

'Old Town Road' feels like a turning point in modern gay rights. A whole generation of young people are growing up with a black, gay hip-hop superstar, proving that there is no space for toxic masculinity in the modern world. It also shows us how things can, and should, evolve, with equal space for fun, creativity and resistance against oppression.

'Dynamite'

BTS (2020)

Question: Does it make any sense to think of the world as 'East' and 'West'?

It must have been 2017, when I was teaching at a school in east London. One of my students in Year 9 was hunched over her exercise book, busily writing. When I drifted over to have a look, I realised that she wasn't doing her schoolwork. She was busy writing words in a language that I couldn't understand.

'What's that?' I asked, more curious than anything. She looked up suddenly like she'd been caught.

'Nothing, sir.'

But after she realised that I had already seen it, she explained.

'It's Korean, sir. I'm learning Korean.'

Now, it's worth noting that this student was not herself Korean, at all. She lived in east London and had Jamaican parents, who also lived in east London. She was a modern British teenager who had never visited Korea in her life. Which made it a bit of a mystery to me as to why she was so busy practising Korean in the middle of her English lesson.

'She's into BTS, sir . . .'

That was the voice of another student on the same table, explaining to me what was going on. The girl in question nodded shyly.

What I didn't know at the time is that BTS was the name of a band. A boy band from South Korea who, unknown to me, had been growing steadily more popular since the 2010s. And because of the internet, their fame had spread out of South Korea into the hearts, minds, mobile phones, laptops and TV screens of young people all over the world. Hence why a young teenager from east London was learning Korean. It turns out she was part of online communities of BTS fans, many of whom spoke Korean, like their pop star idols. I was intrigued.

BTS make a genre of music called *K-pop*, which is short *for Korean popular music*. It's a lively kind of music that comes with dance moves, catchy tunes and screaming fans. It started way back in the 1990s but didn't really take off outside of Asia until the 2010s. One of the biggest K-pop moments was a song called 'Gangnam Style' by a South Korean rapper called Psy. 'Gangnam Style' was ridiculous, infectious, addictive and fun, and it became the first video to reach one billion views on YouTube. Which is amazing.

By 2017, K-pop had become popular enough to be attracting young fans from all over the world.

I have a few theories about this. One important idea is that K-pop is popular because it features a big mix of musical styles. It takes lots of 'Western' music (specifically black American musical styles such as hip-hop, funk, R & B and disco) and fuses them together into this kind of hyperactive super-pop stew. It also comes with incredibly slick music videos, where the singers look beautiful and dance in perfect unison. It's an old pop recipe, with added power for the twenty-first century. In 2018, a BTS song called 'IDOL' leaned further into traditional Korean culture by using instruments such as the *kkwaenggwari* brass gong, the *gakgung* horn and the *janggu* drum. Here, we can see ancient musical styles fused with ultra-modern pop.

In many ways, BTS are K-pop perfection. Their music is smooth and flawless, they dance like Michael Jackson and their videos are full of fun and colour. At the same time, K-pop is influenced by traditional Korean too, which you can hear quietly swimming in the melodies of many K-pop songs, along with all the other styles. For many people, it's an irresistible combination.

Sometimes, the reflection is clearer and brighter than the original image. That's what BTS might represent – an echo of Western pop culture that is somehow louder than the original.

'Dynamite' marks an important moment in K-pop history because it is the first BTS song to reach number one in the USA pop charts. It's also the first BTS song to be written in full English language. It got more than 100 million YouTube views in twenty-four hours (a world record at the time, which proves just how ready the whole world was for a BTS super-song).

Here, we can see the power balance shifting. A lot of this book has been centred on Western music, often originating from the USA. Culturally, the USA has been a big source of popular entertainment for decades – be it music, movies or celebrities. But now, we have huge world superstars coming from a whole other region entirely. Times are changing. Places outside of the West are growing their own superstars, influenced by but not limited to American culture. One clever-sounding word for it is *transnational*, which means crossing nations. Music has always done this, but now, we can see it happening up close, at broadband speeds.

I think this is a good thing. It's a reminder that culture will always spread beyond the pace it was first created and that music, all art, is there to be shared and enjoyed. Different nationalities can feel divided and far apart, almost as though we aren't living on the same rocky planet floating through space. The reality is that for all our differences, we're all the same: something that music allows us to celebrate. And now thirty-nine years after Kyu Sakamoto became the first Asian artist to reach the number one spot in the USA (see page 51) BTS did it again, with a song that exploded, globally.

The chorus to 'Dynamite' talks about being in the stars and setting the night alight, bringing light to the darkness with funk, soul and disco. Pop music might sometimes feel a bit silly and flimsy, but when a pop song really explodes, like dynamite, it can be dazzling and impossible to ignore.

'Woman'

Little Simz featuring Cleo Sol (2021)

Question: What does it feel like to be empowered by your identity?

Two of the biggest things that can define your identity are your race and your gender.

We've travelled a long way through history in this book and the journey has taken us all over the world. And yet, somehow, we haven't managed to shake free of the idea that what our skin looks like, and whether we are male or female, are somehow the most important things about us.

It's strange, when you think about it. That more than two decades into the twenty-first century, the colour of your skin and your sexual biology are still often the first ways that people might choose to describe or define you – even though there is a long list of other factors that we might choose to define ourselves. These include: where we live, where we grew up, our favourite hobbies, what we wear, the music we listen to, when we were born, our jobs, our skills . . . the list is endless. The real problem is that the world that we were all born into (even very old people) has been set up in a way that treats different genders, and different 'races', very differently indeed. (I put 'races' in inverted commas like that because we can accept now that race is a fictional idea that was made up in the 1660s, as a way of splitting people up.)

Simbiatu Abisola Abiola Ajikawo is many things. She's British, and grew up in London. She's a musician who raps and sings. She's an actor too. She comes from a Nigerian heritage. She's what you might call a *millennial*, meaning that she was born between 1981 and 1996. I'm a millennial too, but a much older version (born in 1982).

Like a lot of musicians, Simbiatu is very creative. She has a stage name that works like a nickname, *Little*

Simz, a shortened version of the name 'Simbi'. And in 2021 she released an album called *Sometimes I Might Be Introvert*, with initials that spell out her nickname.

You can see in all of this just how layered and complex Little Simz is, just like every artist featured in this book and just like everyone who ever existed.

At its best, music can offer a window into the lived experiences of all different people. If you are a woman, the way you are treated by the world is different to the way you are treated if you a man. This is called *sexism*, and it is responsible for deeply unfair treatment that girls and women face every day, all over the world and throughout history. If you are racialised as black, you will most likely be treated differently by a world that has been controlled by people who are racialised as white. This is called *racism*, and it has led to inequalities that continue to affect millions of people.

If you are black and female, there are lots of ways that the world might treat you unfairly due to a combination of racism *and* sexism. In Britain, black women often suffer more than their white peers, in a number of different ways. This includes higher levels of stress and difficult mental health, higher risks when pregnant, and low levels of representation across many different jobs. At younger ages, black girls are more likely to be arrested than girls from other ethnic groups, while black Caribbean girls in England are more than twice as likely to be excluded from school than white girls of the same age.

We clearly have a long way to go.

As a song, 'Woman' is a beautifully pure celebration of black women, to black women, from a black woman. It's a smooth, confident song that goes through a list of places that black and brown people come from. Nigeria, Sierra Leone, Tanzania, Ethiopia, Barbados, India, Jamaica, Ghana . . . It's a celebration of beauty, power and intelligence, reminding us that black women are special.

It sounds obvious, but even now, the world is set up in a way that doesn't seem to value black women. One report from 2021 found that black British women are the least likely group in the UK to end up in jobs that earn the most money. The exact reason for this is unknown, but it highlights a basic inequality in the opportunities available for black women to succeed. It also comes alongside other research showing that black women earn less money in their jobs because of sexism and racism combined.

So now that Little Simz picked up a BRIT Award for Best Newcomer in 2022, two years after winning two separate best album awards, alongside a long list of nominations going back to 2016, she really is on her way towards making history. And speaking of history, this is all in a country where the first black female *history* professor was only appointed in 2018 (her name is Olivette Otele, by the way).

We're now getting close to the end of this book. It's a frustrating thing that so many of the injustices we have seen so far are continuing to be seen in the world we share. But the musical world can sometimes be a glimpse of something better. Something more hopeful. In the acceptance speech to her 2022 BRIT award, Little Simz, standing right next to her mum, explained to the world how she started life on a council estate in London. She went on to call the award a blessing, before describing herself as living proof that anyone can achieve anything if they work hard enough. Even if the odds are against you. Even if society is set up to see you fail.

Racism, sexism and all other types of social injustice still exist. We can't just magic them away, but we definitely can dream of something better.

'Patria y Vida'

Yotuel, Gente de Zona, Descemer Bueno, Maykel Osorbo and El Funky (2021)

Question: When does protest turn to power?

Like in a lot of countries, the history of Cuba is full of struggles for power. It must be something about the way power works: the need (or greed) for control can lead to disagreement and conflict. Some of the most famous political struggles in modern history have taken place in Cuba. For this chapter, we need to go back to the middle of the twentieth century.

In 1952, Fulgencio Batista, an army general who led Cuba between 1940 and 1944, used military power to take control of the country and become its leader once again. Seizing power in this way is called a *coup d'état*, a French term going back to the eighteenth century. You might be surprised to find out just how often a *coup* has taken place in different countries at different times throughout history. It's a common way of taking power, relying on physical force and military power.

Batista faced strong challenges to his rule. The strongest opposition came from a revolutionary leader called Fidel Castro who wanted to overthrow Batista's government. In 1958, after six years of pressure, Batista gave up his position. Castro was now Cuba's leader.

Castro's Cuba worried the US government, which wanted South America to be as much like the USA as possible. Remember, at this time in history, the USA was busy establishing itself as a global superpower. The problem was that Castro believed in communism, which the US government did not trust at all. It might sound unimportant, but these disagreements very nearly took the planet into a third world war. One of the biggest communist nations was the Soviet Union, a rival to the USA. Soviet leaders worked closely with

Cuba after Castro took power, which led to serious tensions – especially when Soviet missiles were based on Cuban land.

For most people alive now, these conflicts are the thing of history. As of 2021, Cuba is still led by the Communist Party of Cuba, years after Castro resigned from leadership in 2008.

2021 was a difficult year for people all over the world. In Cuba, the Covid-19 pandemic had created shortages of food and medicine, while strict lockdown rules had put extra pressure on ordinary people. In July that year, tensions bubbled over into the biggest anti-government protests that Cuba had ever seen.

Some people believed that it wasn't just Covid that was making people unhappy, highlighting years of strict communist rule. For protesters, it was all about fairness and opportunity. Standards of living. Human rights. Freedom. And freedom is not a simple thing. Being free of one thing can make you trapped in another. By the 2020s, Cubans who were proud of their country and heritage were also deeply upset with how life in that same country had turned out. There are no easy answers here.

'Patria y Vida' was a huge part of the 2021 Cuban protests. The title of the song translates as *homeland*

and life. It's a powerful phrase – one that calls for opportunity and the chance to live fully and freely in the country you call home.

The song was created by a collaboration of Cuban rappers who wanted to criticise the government. Once again, we see hip-hop being a powerful vehicle for change. 'Patria y Vida' was instantly popular and went viral on the internet. This fact is important. Internet access had only become common in Cuba since 2008, while 3G mobile phone services only arrived in 2019. Without these new technological freedoms, the song might not have spread as quickly as it did.

'Patria y Vida' soon became an anthem as well as a protest slogan in other countries in support of Cuba, including Argentina, Peru and Mexico. It's an emotional song, highlighting injustices and demanding something better, through rap and melody.

Take a moment to think about the power of music to instigate change. Millions of ordinary citizens were united by the words of 'Patria y Vida'. There's a clever line in the chorus that says: *You, five nine; me, double twos*. 'Five nine' refers to 1959; the year that Fidel Castro became the leader of Cuba. At the time, he famously said 'Patria o muerte', which means 'Homeland or death'. These three words would become a slogan for the 1959 Cuban revolution. No one could have predicted that a group of rappers would turn this phrase into a protest slogan against the Cuban government, over sixty years later.

Meanwhile, the phrase 'double twos' refers to 2022, the year that the artists hoped and believed that Cuba would truly become free, and the year in which I began writing this book. The overall message is simple: that for sixty-two years, Cuba had been stuck in a stalemate situation, unable to properly go forward. It's a universal message too, that we have to be free to go forward in the right direction. To live.

In memory of Jamal Edwards

(1990 – 2022)

Sometimes, it's easy to think that you can't make a difference.

Especially if you're young.

It's easy to think that the world is too big, too powerful, for you to change it in any real way. That you have no control over what happens or why.

This is not true.

The truth of the matter is that we are all more powerful, more influential, than we might think. Writing this book has shown me that musical expression can be a weapon in the fight for justice, or (to use a less violent metaphor) a tool we can use to build a better future.

Especially when you are young.

Let me tell you a story about a boy called Jamal.

Jamal lived in London, England, and grew up with his mother, a singer called Brenda. Like a lot of young people, Jamal loved music, but he also loved technology and lots of different ways of being creative, like fashion, videos and computers.

When Jamal turned fifteen, his mother bought him very cool gift. It was a video camera. Now, this was long before the days when everyone has a camera on their phone, and Jamal had a plan. His plan was to use his new camera to film his friends rapping and performing in his local area. Remember, Jamal loves music, so it made sense for him to find young musicians and film their work.

It was around this time, in 2005, that a new website was launched on the internet. You might have heard of it: it's called YouTube. YouTube allowed people to upload videos to share, on something called a YouTube channel. Because YouTube was so new, not many people had heard of it, but young Jamal had a vision. He believed that he could use YouTube to share brilliant music from people just like him, young people who loved music that wasn't being played on the radio or being shown on TV. Young people who were, like Jamal, like me, black – making black music that wasn't supported by big music businesses.

In 2006, Jamal launched his very own channel, called SBTV. (The 'SB' stood for 'Smokey Barz', which was Jamal's rap name). With just his camera and his belief in the talent of people around him, Jamal had started something new. Something that had the potential to be BIG.

Guess what happened next.

SBTV grew. It grew into the biggest platform of its kind for new music from a new generation. Jamal worked incredibly hard on his passion, travelling far and wide to find new talent to film and upload. And he did it because he believed in himself, as well as the talent of others. That was the fuel for this amazing journey that made SBTV the beginning of a revolution in new music. Rap, grime, dance, R & B, UK rap . . . suddenly there was a place for new artists to showcase their talents for the whole world to see.

Jamal Edwards changed the world. He introduced us to hundreds of artists who have contributed to a totally new musical landscape. He believed in their dreams, and built a legacy that has no edges.

- Stormzy
- Dave
- Ed Sheeran
- Emeli Sandé
- Rita Ora
- Jessie J
- Skepta
- Krept and Konan
- Lady Leshurr
- J Hus
- Mic Righteous
- Nines
- Bugzy Malone
- Mist
- Cadet
- Yungen

These are just *some* of the people who Jamal helped to achieve their dreams. Many of them would go on to become some of the biggest, most influential artists in modern British music and some would eventually become international superstars. In fact, there's a whole book to be written about songs from just these artists alone. So, yes, it's safe to say that Jamal Edwards made a difference: to the lives of anyone who is connected in any way to black, British music – which is all of us. Without Jamal's belief, and help, a lot of the music that is taking us into the twenty-first century might never have been made at all.

On 20 February 2022, Jamal Edwards died, at his mother's home in London. There was no way of knowing that it would happen and it came as an incredible shock. Because he had affected so many lives and helped so many people to realise their dreams, literally thousands of messages of support, celebration and grief came pouring in. A day later, I started writing this chapter.

Jamal Edwards died when he was only thirty-one. Not only did he bring musical and creative talent to the world through SBTV, but he also worked to promote awareness of mental health, support young people to find work in creative industries and help build youth centres in Acton, where he grew up.

In 2012, when he was twenty-two, Jamal said something wise and powerful that I think we can all learn from. Listen:

'We all die. The goal isn't to live forever, the goal is to create something that will.'

I want you to think about that. Think about what you believe in, what you love and what you are working towards. For Jamal, it was music and the creative arts, a passion that he shared with everyone he helped to shine. My very first book (which I wrote long after I turned thirty-one) is all about grime, and wouldn't have existed without the stars who Jamal Edwards helped to discover. He wasn't chasing fame or money – he just wanted to help other people and make the world a better place, all through the things that he loved. You can see from all the letters after his name that Jamal was eventually recognised for his work: MBE (Member of the British Empire, awarded by the Queen), MBA (Master of Business Administration – a special business qualification that Jamal was given from a university) and PhD (which refers to a doctorate he was given by another university, in 2021).

That's powerful.

We need to remember people like Jamal Edwards and everything he achieved. He didn't just live in the musical world – he helped build a whole part of it, motivated by passion and a desire to see other people flourish. I dedicate this chapter to Jamal, his family and his long-lasting legacy.

Sharing your story, and being receptive to the stories

of others, will always be one of the most powerful things you can do. This is the true power of music in what can often feel like a divided world. Music is a stream of stories, experiences, feelings, thoughts and ideas. To share that stream and be willing to accept perspectives that seem different to your own is an act of humanity.

There are big problems in this book – some of the biggest you will find in all human history. I'm talking about prejudice and discrimination, war and conflict, death, hatred and greed. The worst aspects of our shared human family. But if you listen to the music that has been created while all this has been happening, across the globe, in different places and different times, you can hear something else entirely. You can hear joy and struggle. Celebration and wisdom. Love and *hope*.

This book is all about hope. It's about the very simple fact that people (most of us) want the world to be a better place. We want things to be fair and we want to see injustice come to an end.

It's amazing to me that you can go on this journey of hope through music alone and, if you pay enough attention, the world of music can help to show you the way.

So.

We've just spent 220 pages and forty songs exploring a whole world of music. We've met countless individuals from countries across the globe, sharing their experiences of the world through melody, rhythm and song. We've skipped through time to the tune of history, making connections between different eras and bringing the past alive in our ears, eyes and hearts. We've gone on a journey through a truly musical world.

And what have we learned?

Some of it has been difficult. How greed and power can lead to people being treated unfairly. How humans can struggle to overcome our many wonderful differences. How old ideas planted long before any of us were born can take centuries to be uprooted. How things like racism, sexism and homophobia can be so difficult to get rid of, even when it's obvious that they add nothing of value to the world. We've also seen how pain and suffering can become the fuel for powerful art, sharing experiences of life that aren't always easy to accept.

But some of it has been so simple. How music can fly above borders and bring people together. How it gives us a universal language that anyone can understand. How pain can be healed by music, and how the stories of the world can be held in a song. Some of the songs you have read about might have been familiar to you, while others might have been new.

When I sat down to write this book, I didn't quite know what it would become. I didn't know all of the stories that I would be putting the spotlight on or all of the people whose names would end up in these pages. *Musical World* has been an act of discovery for me and I hope it has done a similar thing for you. The world is not a perfect place. It never has been and maybe it never will be. But for a few minutes at a time, the beauty of a song can make it all make sense. Think about that the next time you listen to music, whether it's something fast and fun or something slow and serious. Think about how the music makes you feel and how it connects to *your* world. Let yourself be moved. That's what I did while I listened to all these songs, and that's what I hope I've managed to show through my words.

All that's left to say now is *thank you*. Thank you for reading, thank you for listening and thank you for making it this far. The only thing left to do is to keep on exploring. So let's press play, and listen on.

Acknowledgements

First, thank you to all the musicians and artists who provide a soundtrack to our lives. A big thank you also to everyone at Faber who has contributed to bringing this book to life, with a special mention for Leah Thaxton, Bethany Carter and Natasha Brown. Thank you to my agent, Sarah Such of the Sarah Such Literary Agency, for years of support and guidance. And finally, huge thanks to my wife Sophie and my two boys, Finlay and Blake, who I'm privileged to share a whole world of music with (usually dancing around the kitchen).

A *Times* Rock and Pop Music Book of the Year

Musical
Truth

A Musical Journey through Modern Black Britain

'Fantastic.'
Clash Magazine

'Engaging and
accomplished.'
Guardian

JEFFREY BOAKYE
Art by Ngadi Smart

Fancy another walk through musical history?

Music can carry the stories of history like a message in a bottle.

Lord Kitchener, Neneh Cherry, Smiley Culture, Stormzy . . .
Groundbreaking musicians whose songs have changed the world.
But how? This exhilarating playlist tracks some of the key shifts in
modern British history, and explores the emotional impact of 28
songs and the artists who performed them.

This book redefines British history, the Empire and
postcolonialism, and will invite you to think again about
the narratives and key moments in history that you have
been taught up to now.

Thrilling, urgent, entertaining and thought-provoking, this
beautifully illustrated companion to modern black
music is a revelation and a delight.

'It's not just a vital book, but a killer playlist too.'
The Sunday Times